DEVOTED
TO
ISRAEL

MURRAY TILLES

DTI

Roswell, GA

Published by Devoted to Israel, Atlanta, GA

Published in association with Larry Carpenter of Christian Book Services, LLC
www.christianbookservices.com

Cover Design: Josh Feit

Interior Layout Design: Suzanne Lawing

Printed in the United States of America

978-0-9835571-8-0

ENDORSEMENTS

To appreciate and understand the purposes of God in human history means to come to know God's heart for His people, Israel. And God is using my friend Murray Tilles to help us in our understanding of the central place the Jewish people have in the unfolding of God's plan for the ages. As you read through these compelling, insightful devotionals I am sure you will be struck by the unmistakable passion our great God has for His people, our need to pray for the peace of Israel, and the call to lovingly and urgently share the good news of the gospel. Murray, thank you for this gift."

DR. CRAWFORD W. LORITTS, JR.
Author, Speaker, Radio Host
Senior Pastor, Fellowship Bible Church
Roswell, GA

Jesus wept over Israel's lost condition. Paul prayed for Israel's salvation. The British commentator, C. E. B. Cranfield, adds, "In this prayer for Israel's salvation he has set an example for the church to follow. A church which failed to pray for Israel's salvation would be a church which did not know what it means to be the church of Jesus Christ." Murray Tilles wants Christians to have the same heart-felt burden for the Jewish people today, and he's in good company!

JIM R. SIBLEY
Associate Professor and Director of the Pasche
Institute of Jewish Studies at Criswell College

Jesus often prayed for Jerusalem and the Jewish people, and any follower of Jesus can learn more about God's devotion to Israel through these thoughts from Scripture. How has God used the Jewish people in His redemptive plan? How is Israel's experience of faith, failure and forgiveness similar to our own walks with the Lord? How do the holidays of Israel give us cause for celebration today? And how does Israel's future encourage believers about the unfailing promises of God? Murray Tilles guides us through the faithful words of Scripture and encourages us about the faithfulness of God. These devotional thoughts explore truths about the character of God and the role of the Jewish people that, while often neglected in today's church, are found on most of the pages of the Bible. This book will help all of us appreciate God's faithfulness to His promises. Through history, the present, and the future, God is Devoted to Israel.

TIM M. SIGLER, PH.D.
Professor of Hebrew and Biblical Studies
Moody Bible Institute

"Devoted to Israel" is a book that any follower of Jesus should read. It has the right biblical balance between loving the Jewish people and being committed to seeing Israel saved through Jesus the Jewish Messiah. In a day and age where many in the body of Christ are confused when it comes to the subject of Israel, Murray Tilles uses the Bible to bring clarity and to draw one to a correct understanding of the need of the Jewish people for Jesus. As an Israeli Jewish believer in Jesus, and as one actively ministering to the Jewish community here, this book is music to my ears!

DAN SERED
Israel Director
Jews for Jesus

ACKNOWLEDGEMENTS
AND DEDICATION

To my coworkers in Light of Messiah Ministries, Casey and Janine, for the many years of support and encouragement they have given to me.

To Jim Reimann who inspired me to write this devotional, who has encouraged me through the process, and whose editorial work has helped this book be what it is. Our friendship means the world to me.

To my faithful Light of Messiah Ministries board members who walk with me through the joys and challenges of ministry.

To my family who love and know our Messiah, and for my family who have yet to see Him.

To my children, Nathan and Shayna, who are the most wonderful children any father could desire. They have uniquely and wonderfully blessed me with their incredible lives.

To my wife Alana, whose passion for Jesus, love for the Jewish people, and devotion to Israel drew me to her 27 years ago.

To my Lord Jesus, who brought me to Himself, continues to walk with me through the journey of life, and who inspires me to bring His truth to my Jewish people.

FOREWORD

Although raised in a Christian home and neighborhood, my high school was predominantly Jewish. My first job was in a Jewish-owned business, and it was in a stockroom of that very business that I met the Jewish Messiah, who granted me eternal life. Perhaps this is why I've always had a heart for the Jewish people.

Leading tours to Israel at least twice annually for many years has given me increased opportunities to reach out to the Jewish community. It also has given me the opportunity to share with many Gentiles of their responsibility to take the gospel full circle—to take it back to the Jews. Yet many Christians don't fully grasp that responsibility, or if they do, often they are not equipped to reach out to their Jewish friends. In many cases, neither do they know how to pray for them—that is, in a biblical way.

Devoted to Israel, however, is a wonderful, timely tool to remedy these situations. Murray Tilles is a dear friend, and it's Murray's heart for outreach—especially to his Jewish brethren—that so often challenges me to do more to reach the lost, whether in Israel or here at home.

As a Christian, and a devotional author myself, I know the importance of spending time alone with God and His Word. I believe *Devoted to Israel* will help you do that. In the process, not only will it focus your eyes on the Lord and the Jewish people, but also it will give you God's perspective on His chosen ones. My prayer is that it will strengthen your heart to take the gospel back to those to whom we owe so much—the Jewish people. Remember—our Savior—our Messiah—is Jewish! May the Lord grant you His heart for the lost—especially His chosen people—as you read this book.

"My eyes will watch over them for their good, and I will bring them back to this land. I will build them up and not tear them down; I will plant them and not uproot them. I will give them a heart to know me, that I am the LORD. They will be my people, and I will be their God, for they will return to me with all their heart" (Jeremiah 24:6-7).

JIM REIMANN

Jim is the editor of the #1 best-selling, updated editions of *My Utmost for His Highest* and *Streams in the Desert*. His latest books are the updated and expanded editions of Charles Spurgeon's *Morning by Morning* and *Evening by Evening*. He and his wife Pam lead tours of Israel and other Bible lands, which they offer at JimReimann.com.

INTRODUCTION

The Lord has blessed me with the opportunity to speak in several thousand churches around the world, including England, Israel, South Africa, Canada, and every one of the 48 contiguous United States. When speaking, I have also had the blessing of sharing my testimony—how God revealed the Messiah Jesus to me as a Jewish college student in Chapel Hill, NC, through the Old Testament prophecies. In sharing my story, I also have helped others understand the significant place that my Jewish people have in God's heart and plan, and our need to take Jesus back to them. I also have been honored to be a part of seeing many Jewish people receive Jesus as their Messiah. I personally have known Jesus for nearly 33 years.

My great grandparents on my father's side came to the United States from Russia in 1904. My grandparents on my mother's side came from Germany in the 1920s. They were all Jewish. I was raised in a religious Jewish home and instilled with a deep love for my heritage. I have always loved my culture, my people, and my land. Yet when God revealed Himself to me in college, and I gave my life to Him, I experienced the pain of realizing that my parents and most of my family did not understand, and also the pain of seeing most of them reject the Messiah I knew to be true. The Jewish community, for the most part, rejects Jesus as Messiah. I have spent 28 years taking the message of Jesus back to the people whom I love so dearly.

Wherever I speak I experience wonderful people who love and care deeply about the Jewish community, about Israel, and are fascinated with the Jewish roots of our faith. Of this I am grateful. Many Christians, including Christian leaders, are getting involved in a growing movement to support Israel. Of that I am also grateful. We must strongly stand in support of the Jewish homeland. In the process, however, we must also keep perspective. The proclamation of the gospel must come first—in tandem, with our support of Israel—because peace won't come until Jesus reigns in individual hearts and returns to establish His Kingdom.

Most Christians are aware of the passages in Scripture that say, "I will bless those who bless you" (Gen. 12:3), and "Pray for the peace of Jerusalem" (Ps. 122:6). However, most Christians know very little about the land and the people who are so deeply loved by God. We are interested but neglect to pray. We also neglect to share the good news. Our limited knowledge can only take us so far. We have to allow our heart to be knitted together with God's. He has a special love for Israel, for Jerusalem, and for my Jewish people. Our hearts need to turn in that direction as well.

I have written this devotional because of my love for my people, and because I know that prayer is effective. I believe that God wants the Christian community to pray for Israel and for the Jewish community. Understanding more about Israel, the Jewish people, and our Jewish roots should place a burden on our hearts—a burden to pray AND to take the incredible message of Jesus back to them.

It is my hope and prayer that this devotional will inspire and encourage more Christians to pray for the people who have that special place in God's heart and plan. I am hoping that more prayers will go up to God for the peace of Jerusalem. And, in the process, it is my hope that you will learn more about the city that Jesus wept over and the people whom He desires to gather together under His wings. Please take your time with this book. Do not rush through it. It is not meant to be read through from beginning to end in a day, or even a few days. Ponder the message of each devotion and let it speak to you personally. Extend each prayer. Pray each one asking God to do a work in your heart. It is my sincere hope that He will do just that.

As I have written this devotional, I have often spoken in the first person. The Jewish people are literally "my people." I have not stopped being Jewish. I am one of them, and I love them. I cry out along with my brother, the apostle Paul: "My heart's desire and prayer to God for the Israelites is that they may be saved" (Rom. 10:1). My people need the Messiah—they need Jesus. He has come.

May the church's burden be to take the message of hope and peace in our Messiah back to the community who gave us our Messiah, and may that burden continually grow. I hope this devotional helps you along your journey, as you love Israel and my Jewish people.

For the sake of Israel,

MURRAY TILLES

DEVOTED TO ISRAEL

WITH PRAISE AND THANKSGIVING THEY
SANG TO THE LORD:
"HE IS GOOD; HIS LOVE TO ISRAEL
ENDURES FOREVER."

EZRA 3:1 1

Most people know Jesus was Jewish and lived a Jewish life. A majority of Christians also know that Israel is an important place. From the time we are children we hear about the Israelites as we learn the Bible stories—stories all set in and around the land of Israel. Christians often say, "We are indebted to the Jewish people," and, "They are God's chosen ones." Anyone who really knows Jesus deeply and intimately has a place in their heart for the Jewish people. If you love Jesus, you have to love the Jewish community, for He was one of them.

Unfortunately, for nearly 2000 years, one of the reasons the Jewish people have not come to know Jesus is that many who say they love Him have also hated them. A reality of our misguided church history is that the church has not, for the most part, shown love for Jewish people or Israel. My people have died at the hands of "Crusaders for Christ," saying they wanted to rid the world of the Jews so that the purity of "Christianity" could prevail. And yet, Jesus was Jewish, Paul was Jewish, and the New Testament itself was written by Jewish authors.

Today, however, there is a movement within evangelical Christianity to turn back the clock. More and more Christians are showing their love and devotion to the Jewish community and to Israel. Some even say we should repent for the past sins of the church. Yet this movement can be misguided as well, for it is a movement that oftentimes expresses love for Israel and the Jewish people, while neglecting or resisting to share Jesus with them. We cannot truly love the Jewish people and Israel without bringing them the gospel message of Jesus. To be fully devoted to Israel means to stand with Israel the nation, to love the Jewish people, but most importantly, to bring the message of Jesus back to those who brought Him to us. If we are devoted to Israel, we will tell them about Jesus. Devotion to the land and the people without devotion to the message of the gospel and the gift of salvation in Messiah Jesus—"to the Jew first" (Rom. 1:16, KJV)—is not devotion at all.

PRAYER

God of Israel, help me to know what loving Israel truly means. Help me to love them with Your love. Help me to see them through Your eyes. Open my heart and my mind to understand Your deep devotion to Israel so I may love them the way You do. Your love for Israel endures forever. Give me a burden to not only love them, but also to show them love by bringing them the gospel and helping them to see Jesus through my love. In Messiah's Name, Amen.

ONLY ONE CITY

PRAY FOR THE PEACE OF JERUSALEM: MAY THOSE
WHO LOVE YOU BE SECURE.

PSALM 122:6

There is only one city that the Bible says to pray for: Jerusalem. In fact, an entire Psalm is devoted to the city of Jerusalem. It is the city whose gates are to be praised, and is the city where the tribes of Israel would go up to worship the God of Abraham, Isaac, and Jacob. King David made it the capital of the united kingdom of Israel 1000 years before Jesus. It is the city God chose for His home, and His house—the temple—was built on its highest hill.

God loves Jerusalem, and the prayer of the Psalmist is that God's people who also truly love Jerusalem may dwell in security. It should be a city of peace, but unfortunately, it has been a city surrounded by conflict for thousands of years. The Babylonians, Syrians, and Romans, just to name a few, have invaded it and laid claim to it. Today the world waits in anticipation, wondering what is going to happen to the city in the future.

Jerusalem has been a center of conflict because it is in the center of God's plan. Because it plays a significant role in God's future revelation of His glory and kingdom, Jerusalem attracts the attention of the Enemy who wants to thwart His plan. But those of us who know Messiah Jesus know He is going to return to Jerusalem to establish His kingdom of peace. He wept over the city of Jerusalem, left from the city of Jerusalem, and is going to return to the city of Jerusalem to rule and reign. One day, peace will come to it in the form of a person—the Messiah Jesus. There will not be any peace there until He returns to establish His kingdom. So we pray that peace will come and that people will receive the true peace of God, which can be found in the person of Jesus—and in Him alone.

PRAYER

Lord God in heaven, I "pray for the peace of Jerusalem." You love that city. It is Yours, and it is special. Please protect Your city and the people who dwell there. Help those who do not yet know You, to come to know You. Messiah Jesus, open the eyes of those who need to see. Bring peace to Your city. "Come quickly" (Rev. 22:20, KJV), Lord Jesus, and establish your kingdom. In Messiah's Name, Amen.

JERUSALEM—CHOSEN BY GOD

SINCE THE DAY I BROUGHT MY PEOPLE OUT OF EGYPT, I
HAVE NOT CHOSEN A CITY IN ANY TRIBE OF ISRAEL TO
HAVE A TEMPLE BUILT FOR MY NAME TO BE THERE,
NOR HAVE I CHOSEN ANYONE TO BE THE LEADER
OVER MY PEOPLE ISRAEL. BUT NOW I HAVE CHOSEN
JERUSALEM FOR MY NAME TO BE THERE, AND I HAVE
CHOSEN DAVID TO RULE MY PEOPLE ISRAEL.

2 CHRONICLES 6:5-6

Solomon, David's son, after being given wisdom from God, gave orders to build a temple for the Name of the Lord. It is strange to think that God went on a search for a home, but He did. He wasn't searching in a human sense, but was waiting for the opportune time and place. After the commandments on stone tablets were given to Moses on Mount Sinai, and the Ark of the Covenant was built, God had no true resting place. His Presence wandered with the Israelites through the wilderness. He was with them, but was always on the move. He dwelt with them, leading them by His presence through "the pillar of cloud by day" and "the pillar of fire by night" (Ex. 13:22)—God moving with His people.

Later God chose Jerusalem for His home—a city set on a high hill. Some 70,000 men worked as carriers on its construction, another 80,000 were stonecutters, and still another 3,600 were foremen over them. (See 2 Chron. 2:2.) Skilled craftsmen who worked with gold and silver; bronze and iron; and in purple, crimson, and blue yarn were employed to build and decorate the house of the Lord. The temple was constructed so that it would be greater than all the other houses of worship ever known to mankind. Solomon said, "The temple I am going to build will be great, because our God is greater than all other gods" (2 Chron. 2:5).

Today we wait for the *rebuilding* of the house of God, and it will be accomplished. Though the nations conspire against the City of God and the reign of Messiah on His throne, one day the temple will be rebuilt, and Jesus will live there. Although His house was once torn down—just as He prophesied in Mark 13:2: "Not one stone here will be left on another; every one will be thrown down"—it is going to rise again one day. Messiah will inhabit it and will reign as King of Kings and Lord of Lords.

PRAYER

God of creation, You chose Your house and that house was set on a hill in the city of Jerusalem. Though the Temple Mount is desolate today, Your home destroyed, and its stones torn down, I look forward to its rebuilding. I desperately wait in anticipation for Jesus to return, to establish Your kingdom, and to take His place on the throne of David. Today I pray for Your soon return to Jerusalem, Jesus. In Your Mighty Name, Amen.

THE ANCIENT CONFLICT BEGINS

YOU SHALL NAME HIM ISHMAEL, FOR THE LORD HAS HEARD OF YOUR MISERY. HE WILL BE A WILD DONKEY OF A MAN; HIS HAND WILL BE AGAINST EVERYONE AND EVERYONE'S HAND AGAINST HIM, AND HE WILL LIVE IN HOSTILITY TOWARD ALL HIS BROTHERS.

GENESIS 16:11-12

Most people do not understand that the conflict we are witnessing today in the Middle East is not a modern conflict, but is an ancient conflict rooted in biblical history. The beginning of the conflict is recorded in Genesis chapters 16 and 21, where we read of the births of Ishmael and Isaac, the two sons of Abraham through whom were born the descendants who are at odds with one another even today. The Islamic community claims ancestry back to Abraham through Ishmael. The Jewish people, the Israelites, claim ancestry back to Abraham through Isaac. The birth of these two sons, and the enmity between them, has continued more than 4,000 years, up to the present time.

In Genesis 16 we read the story of Ishmael and God's description of him. "Then the angel of the LORD told her, 'Go back to your mistress and submit to her.'" The angel added, "I will increase your descendants so much that they will be too numerous to count." He also said, "You are now pregnant and you will give birth to a son. You shall name him Ishmael, for the LORD has heard of your misery. He will be a wild donkey of a man; his hand will be against everyone and everyone's hand against him, and he will live in hostility toward all his brothers" (Genesis 16:9-12). Later we see in Genesis 21:9 that at the weaning ceremony of Isaac, Sarah saw that Ishmael was "mocking" Isaac.

The current conflict between Israel and its neighbors today is simply an extension of the ancient conflict that began with the birth of Ishmael and Isaac. It should not surprise us that wars rage around the world to this day, for war and conflict are a result of the fall of humanity in the Garden of Eden. Hatred, genocide, cruel governments and leaders, are the result of our lost condition and the sinful nature of man. We should be even less surprised that biblically and historically the world's attention is continually drawn back to the Middle East, to Israel, and to Jerusalem—the place where it all began.

PRAYER

God of Abraham, Isaac, and Jacob, I know that the conflict that rages today in the Middle East grieves Your heart and yet I also know it does not surprise You. You knew it was going to happen. I thank You that You are sovereign over the conflict which began as two brothers and their descendants began to squabble and fight, yet You told us they would live in conflict. I ask You to intervene, to protect, and to make Yourself known to those in the Middle East who do not yet know You. Bring them Your peace. I rest, knowing You are in control. In Messiah's Name, Amen.

THE ANCIENT CONFLICT CONTINUES

WE HIS SERVANTS WILL START REBUILDING, BUT AS
FOR YOU, YOU HAVE NO SHARE IN JERUSALEM OR ANY
CLAIM OR HISTORIC RIGHT TO IT."
NEHEMIAH 2:20

The ancient conflict that began in Genesis 16 and 21 continued throughout Scripture. The enmity between the brothers escalated, therefore, the animosity between the Israelites and the nations surrounding never stopped. The Egyptians, Caananites, Philistines, Ammonites, Moabites, and Babylonians, just to name a few, attempted to destroy the Jewish people. Yet throughout the conflict God has shown His faithfulness to Israel and to the Jewish.people. Though He prophesized that the conflict would continue, He has always used it to further His purpose and plan.

The prophet Nehemiah was called as God's servant to rebuild the walls of Jerusalem that had been torn down and burned by the Babylonians (the modern-day Iraqis). The conflict surrounding Jerusalem continued. Nehemiah and the Israelites committed in their hearts to rebuild the special ancient city of God and the temple. They knew that the defamation of the city of Jerusalem meant the defamation of the Name of God Himself. God's house disgraced—God disgraced—thus, God's people disgraced.

The Israelites desired to obey God, but opposition raised its head in the form of leaders from the surrounding nations. After committing to rebuild the walls of Jerusalem, the Israelites were faced with scorn from their enemies. "When Sanballat the Horonite, Tobiah the Ammonite official, and Geshem the Arab [Persian/Iranian] heard about it, they mocked and ridiculed us. 'What is this you are doing?' they asked, 'Are you rebelling against the king?' [Nehemiah] answered them by saying, 'The God of heaven will give us success. We his servants will start rebuilding, but as for you, you have no share in Jerusalem or any claim or historic right to it'" (Neh. 2:19-20).

Jerusalem belongs to the Israelites—to the Jewish people. The surrounding nations have no share in it, claim to it, or historic right to it. Though the nations today continue to squabble over the land of Israel and the city of Jerusalem, God tells us in His Word, that the land and the city are His. And He has given them to the Jewish people. It cannot, and should not, ever be divided again.

PRAYER

Dear God of Abraham, Isaac, and Jacob, as the nations surrounding Israel attempt to divide Your land and city, please protect and defend Your people. Please give wisdom to the leaders of Israel and open the eyes of those who may have the intent to divide what is Yours. Please hinder those who would try to take Jerusalem from its rightful heirs. I thank you for your protection. In Messiah's Name, Amen.

✡

THE ANCIENT CONFLICT ENDS

THEN THE LORD WAS JEALOUS FOR HIS LAND
AND TOOK PITY ON HIS PEOPLE.

JOEL 2:18

Though the conflict between Israel and its neighbors has continued through the millennia, and continues still today, God promises an end to the conflict. One day it will come to a conclusion. God gives us a preliminary picture of that day as we read of the judgment of the nations surrounding Israel by the prophet Zephaniah. After the judgment of Israel and Judah—a judgment intended to restore them—there will be judgment of the nations that surround Israel—a judgment intended for destruction. In the end, the nations who are intent on destroying Israel will be destroyed themselves.

In Zephaniah we read, "I have heard the insults of Moab and the taunts of the Ammonites, who insulted my people and made threats against their land. ... Gaza will be abandoned and Ashkelon left in ruins. At midday Ashdod will be emptied and Ekron uprooted. Woe to you who live by the sea, O Kerethite people; the word of the LORD is against you, Canaan, land of the Philistines, I will destroy you and none will be left. ... This is what they will get in return for their pride, for insulting and mocking the people of the LORD Almighty." (Zeph. 2:8, 4-5, 10)

There is a biblical principle wrapped up in these few verses. Any individual or group of people who have as a part of their agenda the persecution of the Jewish people or the destruction of Israel will come to their own destruction. Because God promises to protect the Jewish people, and because He has promised the land of Israel to the Jewish people, anyone who comes against those plans will be destroyed themselves. This principle is a warning to any nation who would be a part of the division of the land of Israel or the city of Jerusalem. God will not be mocked and will not be called a liar. He will keep His promises, and one day those who come against His promises will come to their own destruction as they battle the God of Abraham, Isaac, and Jacob. It is not wise to throw dirt, especially "holy" dirt, in the face of the Creator of the universe.

PRAYER

God help me to have Your heart for Israel. Help me to always stand with the Jewish people and nation You love so much. Please help the leaders of our nation, and of all nations, to stand with—not against—the land and city You wept over. Strengthen Israel in her struggle and open the eyes of all who would wage war against her. In Messiah Jesus' Name, Amen.

JERUSALEM—CENTRAL TO THE CONFLICT

I WILL MAKE KNOWN MY HOLY NAME AMONG MY PEOPLE ISRAEL. I WILL NO LONGER LET MY HOLY NAME BE PROFANED, AND THE NATIONS WILL KNOW THAT I THE LORD AM THE HOLY ONE IN ISRAEL. IT IS COMING! IT WILL SURELY TAKE PLACE, DECLARES THE SOVEREIGN LORD. THIS IS THE DAY I HAVE SPOKEN OF.
EZEKIEL 39:7-8

The end of the conflict will come when the nations surround Jerusalem, intent on making war and destroying it. Though the eyes of the world may be on individual conflicts within the Middle East, the greater concern is over stability of the entire Middle East and how it is going to affect Israel. Egypt and Jordan are the only countries in the Middle East that have maintained peace with Israel. And Israel is the only country in the Middle East that has a democratic form of government, which represents freedom for its citizens. The question we should be asking is: As Middle Eastern governments are replaced, who is going to fill the vacuum, and how will that affect Israel?

One thing is certain. At some point in the future the entire world is going to wage war against Israel, and even more specifically, against Jerusalem. Yet Israel will stand alone. As believers we watch what is happening around the world, but we do not have to wonder in darkness. The stage is being set. The turmoil throughout the Middle East today is one small piece in a much larger puzzle. But God has shown us the full picture. We can stand back and look at the painting. Rather than seeing it in part, we can see it in its fullness. God is at work, and Jerusalem is central to the conflict. Here is God's prophecy given through Zechariah:

"A prophecy: The word of the LORD concerning Israel. ... 'I am going to make Jerusalem a cup that sends all the surrounding peoples reeling. Judah will be besieged as well as Jerusalem. On that day, when all the nations of the earth are gathered against her, I will make Jerusalem an immovable rock for all the nations. All who try to move it will injure themselves. On that day I will strike every horse with panic and its rider with madness,' declares the LORD. ... Then the clans of Judah will say in their hearts, 'The people of Jerusalem are strong, because the LORD Almighty is their God'" (Zech. 12:1-5).

The conflict throughout the Middle East is setting the stage for the final battle—one that will culminate in the return of Jesus. As the world watches the unfolding events and wonders what is going to happen next, we wait in anticipation for the return of Jesus to His throne in Jerusalem.

PRAYER

Abba, Father, thank you for Your Son Jesus. I know that in the end, after the nations come against Your land and Your people, Messiah is going to return. He is going to return as King of Kings. He will return at the sound of a trumpet, as the Lion of Judah, to establish His kingdom. Maranatha! "Come quickly" (Rev. 22:20, KJV), *Lord Jesus. In Your name, Amen.*

The Only Solution to the Conflict

Peace I leave with you; my peace I give you.
I do not give you as the world gives.
Do not let your hearts be troubled and
do not be afraid.

John 14:27

Instability in the Middle East is nothing new. The region has been unstable from the beginning of time, as recorded in the Scriptures. The nations have labored in vain to find a solution to the problem. Some have tried to wipe out Israel and the Jewish people, hoping their demise would mean peace for the world, while others have tried governing the region from afar. President after president in the U.S. has made peace in the Middle East a goal for his tenure, which would be the crown jewel of accomplishments for any world leader who believes in freedom and democracy. The United Nations has attempted to bring peace to the Middle East as well. Yet every attempt has failed.

No amount of geopolitical maneuvering or strategic political savvy can bring peace to the Middle East, because the problem is not a geopolitical one. Nor is the problem a diplomatic one at its core. Because the world does not understand the root of the conflict, our leaders strive to find answers to the problem without understanding the cause. It is like trying to treat a viral infection with antibiotics. It cannot be done, because viruses do not respond to antibiotics, only bacteria do.

Conflict in the Middle East began as a spiritual problem and can only be solved through spiritual means. The animosity between the descendants of Ishmael and the descendants of Isaac began as a result of sin and disobedience. That animosity will continue on a grand scale until Jesus brings His peace to the nations. Until then, peace can only come on an individual level, not nationally.

The only way to have lasting peace in Israel is to bring individual Muslims and Jewish people to Jesus. Peace is not the absence of conflict, but is the presence of God. Jesus is the "Prince of Peace" (Isa. 9:6). When He returns, peace will come to the world in a person who is "KING OF KINGS AND LORD OF LORDS" (Rev. 19:16). He will reign and my people will see. Everyone will see.

PRAYER

God of Shalom—God of peace—I know that you will bring Your peace to the Middle East. I also know that true peace can only come in the form of the person, Jesus. Give me hope and comfort today, knowing that You are the sovereign God of peace. Help me to be mindful today to remember to pray for those in the Middle East who do not yet know You, that they would give their hearts to You—both Jewish and Muslim people. In Messiah's Name, Amen.

ON THAT DAY

I WILL POUR OUT ON THE HOUSE OF DAVID AND THE
INHABITANTS OF JERUSALEM A SPIRIT OF GRACE AND
SUPPLICATION. THEY WILL LOOK ON ME, THE ONE THEY
HAVE PIERCED, AND THEY WILL MOURN FOR HIM AS ONE
MOURNS FOR AN ONLY CHILD, AND GRIEVE BITTERLY
FOR HIM AS ONE GRIEVES FOR A FIRSTBORN SON.

ZECHARIAH 12:10

On the day of the final, end-times attack, something amazing is going to happen. My people are going to see Jesus! The nations will surround Israel and Jerusalem intent upon bringing peace to the world in their own way. With Israel surrounded, and the nations attacking, everything will seem hopeless. But then Jesus returns. At that moment—at the very last moment—at the sound of a shofar, the Trumpet of God, He is going to split the sky. His feet will touch down on the Mount of Olives. He is going to walk down the hill, cross the Kidron Valley, walk up the hill of the Temple Mount, and finally take His place in the temple. He is going to sit down on His throne and judge with fairness and righteousness. Jesus will establish His earthly kingdom.

My people will look and they will mourn. They will see, but with astonishment, thinking to themselves, "It was Jesus all along!" Even though many may interpret Zechariah 12:10 in a way that indicates a universal salvation for the Jewish people on that day, this verse in no way communicates that. Neither does it communicate that Jewish people get a second chance at salvation in the future. There is no retroactive acceptance into the kingdom of God after one dies, for "just as people are destined to die once, and after that to face judgment" (Heb. 9:27). But one day in the future there will be a national restoration of my Jewish people to our Messiah. They will see and fully understand, as a nation and community, that Jesus truly is our Messiah! Until then we watch, we wait, we pray, we work.

PRAYER

Author of Creation, open the eyes of those who need to see Your truth in the Middle East. I pray for Jewish people to accept their Messiah. I pray for Muslims to say "yes" to the "Prince of Peace" (Isa. 9:6)—to say "yes" to Jesus. I pray for Jerusalem and for the land of Israel. Protect her and bring her peace. I look forward to the day when You return, when all Israel will look upon You, and when You cleanse them from their sin. In Jesus' Name, Amen.

FOR HIS GLORY

THEN THE CLANS OF JUDAH WILL SAY IN THEIR HEARTS, "THE PEOPLE OF JERUSALEM ARE STRONG, BECAUSE THE LORD ALMIGHTY IS THEIR GOD."

ZECHARIAH 12:5

Surrounding Jerusalem in an attempt to bring peace to the world is the plan of the nations, but God will be waiting for them with His plan, for He is the sovereign Lord of creation. Jerusalem is where He promises to bring the conflict to its conclusion. The nations will surround the land of Israel and the city of Jerusalem, thinking their solution will solve the world's problems. And just as it has been throughout history, the destruction of the Jewish people will be seen as the solution. But God says, in essence, "Bring it on!"

In the following verses from Ezekiel, God explains why He is orchestrating world events in this way: "This is what the sovereign LORD says: It is not for your sake, people of Israel, that I am going to do these things, but for the sake of my holy name, which you have profaned among the nations where you have gone. I will show the holiness of my great name, which has been profaned among the nations, the name you have profaned among them. Then the nations will know that I am the LORD, ...when I am proved holy through you before their eyes" (Ezek. 36:22-23).

God is a jealous God who desires His creation to recognize His authority. The Scriptures reveal that His plan is to use a tiny nation, surrounded by the world, standing all alone, to show His power. Isn't it just like God to whittle circumstances down to the point where only He can be seen through them? Just as He ordained for Gideon's army to dwindle from 32,000 to 300, and little David to defeat the entire Philistine army with a few smooth stones, so God will bring about the establishment of His kingdom through little Israel, surrounded by the world.

PRAYER

God, you are a God who works through the smallest group. You do not need a mighty army to accomplish Your purposes, because You are the greatest of commanders. You are the Lord of Hosts! Thank You that You promised to protect Israel. As the nations gather around her, You promised to defend her so that, in the end, You will be shown the powerful and faithful God of Your covenantal promises. And thank You that even in our lives You cause our circumstances to sometimes become seemingly hopeless so that You might be given the glory in their resolution. In Jesus' Name, Amen.

THE NEW TESTAMENT

IF SOMEONE ELSE THINKS THEY HAVE REASONS TO
PUT CONFIDENCE IN THE FLESH, I [THE APOSTLE PAUL]
HAVE MORE: CIRCUMCISED ON THE EIGHTH DAY, OF
THE PEOPLE OF ISRAEL, OF THE TRIBE OF BENJAMIN,
A HEBREW OF HEBREWS; IN REGARD TO THE LAW, A
PHARISEE; ... AS FOR RIGHTEOUSNESS BASED ON
THE LAW, FAULTLESS.

PHILIPPIANS 3: 4-6

As a young Jewish college student wondering about my relationship with God, I naturally began to read the Jewish Bible, or what we call the Old Testament. It was the only book I knew to read. I was searching the Scriptures, trying to understand the truth of God. In His sovereignty, He placed some Christians across the hall from me in my dormitory. They invited me to a Bible study and began to ask me questions about Jewish beliefs. Having been raised in a religious Jewish home, I was easily able to answer them.

During one of our visits they asked if I had ever read any of the messianic prophecies found in the Old Testament. After telling them that I hadn't, they pointed me in the direction of the ancient prophecies that talk of the coming of Messiah. As I read, it seemed those prophecies spoke of Jesus, so I decided to begin reading the New Testament as well.

I had expected that the New Testament was a book written by and for

Christians. But I was in for quite a shock! As I began to read, I saw that the New Testament words, phrases, thoughts, and ideas were all Jewish. I began to understand that Jesus lived a Jewish life, that He was a rabbi, that all of the writers of the New Testament (with the possible exception of Luke) were Jewish. I also realized that nearly everyone who believed in Jesus while He was on Earth, was Jewish. It wasn't long before I came to fully grasp that the New Testament is a Jewish book, written in a Jewish context, about an internal Jewish struggle. It can't get more Jewish than that!

After coming to that realization, I became a believer in Jesus as Messiah. One night in the quietness of my own room I asked Jesus into my life. In my mind, I was accepting the Jewish Messiah—the fulfillment of our prophets' hopes and expectations. I was doing a very Jewish thing! In fact, the most Jewish thing anyone can do is to accept Jesus as Messiah. He is *our* Rabbi!

PRAYER

Jesus, thank you for being my Rabbi. Thank you for grafting me into this rich heritage. Help me to learn more about my Jewish roots, the Jewish people, and the land of Israel—the land You love so much. I am blessed because of the Jewish people. Through them I have been given the ultimate gift in You, my Savior. Help me to love them more. In Your Name I pray, Amen.

עשן בני גרשון ובני מררי נשאי לאשי הלמישכן ומסע...
כל מולנה ראובן לצבאתם ועל צבאו אליצור
שדיאור ועל צבא מטה בני שמעון שלמיא
צורישדי ועל צבא מטה בני זר אליסף בן
עואל ונסעו הקהתים נשאי המקדש והקימו
ת המשכן עד באם ונסעו דגל מחנה בני אפרי
צבאתם ועל צבאו אלישמע בן עמיהוד ועל
בא מטה בני מנשה גמליאל בן פדהצור ועל
בא מטה בני בנימן אבידן בן גדעוני ונסע דגל
חנה בני דן מאסף לכל המחנת לצבאתם וע...

THE JEWISH PEOPLE— CHOSEN FOR A PURPOSE

THE NATIONS WILL SEE YOUR VINDICATION, AND ALL KINGS YOUR GLORY; YOU WILL BE CALLED BY A NEW NAME THAT THE MOUTH OF THE LORD WILL BESTOW. YOU WILL BE A CROWN OF SPLENDOR IN THE LORD'S HAND, A ROYAL DIADEM IN THE HAND OF YOUR GOD.

ISAIAH 62:2-3

God chose the Jewish people to be His first ambassadors to the world. In Deuteronomy we read that He chose the Jewish people because He desired to do so, due to His love for them. There is no other explanation. The passage states, "The LORD did not set his affection on you and choose you because you were more numerous than other peoples, for you were the fewest of all peoples. But it was because the LORD loved you and kept the oath he swore to your ancestors that he brought you out with a mighty hand and redeemed you from the land of slavery" (Deut. 7:7-8).

The Jewish people were chosen because God loved them, and they were His "first loved" people. Their ambassadorship included the receiving of the law, the writing of the Scriptures, and the establishment of the worship of the one true God of Abraham, Isaac, and Jacob.

Though my people continually struggled in their position of being God's chosen ones, it was through the Jewish people that God chose to bring forth His truth to the pagan world. Even through slavery and bondage, through judgment and discipline, God used the Jewish people as His example to the world.

Yet today's Jewish community does not seek converts to Judaism. Though they were called to bring the nations into a relationship with the God of Abraham, Isaac, and Jacob, the modern Jewish position is that each person has his or her own way to God. Furthermore, they believe that each person's way is fine as long as he or she believes in one God and does not hurt others. This change in the rabbis' teachings has come as a result of thousands of years of persecution and the desire to be accepted. Thus, in an attempt to be accepted, they accept.

Modern Judaism has failed in its biblical mission to reach the world with the message of God. However, the Jewish community's failure [transgression] meant Messiah came for all. Thus, all who believe become His ambassadors—His representatives to take the truth of the God of Israel to the world.

PRAYER

Father, thank You that although You called the Jewish people to take Your truth to the world, and that although they have not been obedient, You still made a way. You sent our Messiah to bear our sins and called Gentiles as well to come into Your kingdom, become Your ambassadors, and to share in Your inheritance. Thank You for using me, and please help me to proclaim Your truth today. I am Your ambassador in Messiah Jesus. In His Name, Amen.

THE JEWISH PEOPLE ARE STILL GOD'S CHOSEN PEOPLE

WHAT ADVANTAGE, THEN, IS THERE IN BEING A JEW, OR WHAT VALUE IS THERE IN CIRCUMCISION? MUCH IN EVERY WAY! FIRST OF ALL, THE JEWS HAVE BEEN ENTRUSTED WITH THE VERY WORDS OF GOD.

ROMANS 3:1-2

The apostle Paul states in Romans 11:28-29, "As far as the gospel is concerned, [the Jews] are enemies on your account; but as far as election is concerned, they are loved on account of the patriarchs, for God's gifts and his call are irrevocable." Though, for the most part, the Jewish people have rejected Jesus as Messiah and turned their backs on God, they still have a special place in His heart. They have not been rejected by God or cast away because of their unbelief.

Though they are still God's chosen people, they have failed in their initial mission, and that baton has been passed on to all of those who believe in Jesus, whether Jew or Gentile. Believers in Jesus are God's current chosen ones to take His truth to an unbelieving world. Those of us who know Jesus have been given the gospel, and it is now our mission and obligation to reach the world with the message of hope, truth, and salvation in Jesus, the Messiah. But our chosen position in no way cancels out or negates the chosen position of the Jewish people, which came as a covenant from God that has not, and will not, be broken.

Their chosen status remains because God's promises are still in effect. God said He would protect the Jewish people, bring them back to their land, restore their nation, increase their numbers, and restore their fortunes. Those promises have not been revoked even though they have, for the most part, rejected Jesus as the Messiah. Their chosen status is not dependent upon their obedience to God, but upon God's obedience to His own Word—something He will never break. He made promises to the Jewish people that He is keeping, and will keep, into the future. The greatest of those promises is Messiah's promise to return, to establish His kingdom among them, and to show them salvation. When Jesus returns, my people will see.

Rejection of Jesus by some, or most, Jewish people in no way affects their chosen position as the people through whom God brought His truth to the world. They truly are enemies of God for the sake of the gospel, but they are elected and loved "on account of the patriarchs"—a people who still have a special place in God's heart. His promises, His call, and His faithfulness is unchanging and cannot be called back. Aren't you glad?

PRAYER

Abba Father, thank You for calling the Jewish people. Though, as a community, they have rejected Your provision of Jesus, they are still loved by You. Help us to love them as You do. Help me to remember that Your "gifts and ... call are irrevocable" for them, and for me. I love You. In Your precious Name, Amen.

BEING CHOSEN— UNQUALIFIED ACCESS INTO HEAVEN?

AS FAR AS THE GOSPEL IS CONCERNED, THEY
ARE ENEMIES ON YOUR ACCOUNT; BUT AS FAR AS
ELECTION IS CONCERNED, THEY ARE LOVED ON
ACCOUNT OF THE PATRIARCHS, FOR GOD'S GIFT AND
HIS CALL ARE IRREVOCABLE.
ROMANS 11:28-29

Unfortunately, there are some in the evangelical church who confuse being "chosen" with being "saved." Some say the Jewish people automatically have a relationship with God based on the covenant God made with them through Abraham. This statement could not be further from the truth. The Jewish community's chosen position does not mean they have an immediate, unqualified entrance into heaven.

Many think that because the Jewish people were chosen by God that they are all biblically literate and automatically have a relationship with God. No! We are all separated from God by sin, for "there is no one who does good, not even one" (Ps. 14:3). And in Isaiah we read, "Your iniquities have separated you from your God; your sins have hidden his face from you" (Isa. 59:2). Thus, "chosen" does not equal "saved."

Just like anyone else, Jewish people need Jesus to know God and to go to heaven. They need the Good News to be proclaimed to them. Jesus said, "I am the way and the truth and the life. No one comes to the Father except through me" (John 14:6); while Peter, a Jewish disciple, proclaimed to the Jewish supreme court of his day, "There is no other name under heaven given to men by which we must be saved" (Acts 4:12). The message of salvation is clear. Jesus is the only way.

Often Christians are taught, or assume, that the Jewish people have a special "in" to heaven. There is an assumption that Jewish people get a second chance, or that they can enter heaven through their religious works of righteousness. Of course, Jesus was clear—the Bible is clear—there is no other way to heaven except through Jesus. All who are saved and go to heaven get there the same way: "For it is by grace you have been saved, through faith—and this not from yourselves, it is the gift of God—not by works, so that no one can boast" (Eph. 2:8-9).

PRAYER

God of salvation, thank You that my relationship with You is not dependent upon my goodness. You accept me and give me a relationship with You by faith, due to Your grace. Help me to be true to Your gospel. There is no other way to You except through Messiah who died for my sins. Help me to remember that Jewish people need Jesus too. In His Name, Amen.

THE JEWISH PEOPLE— CHOSEN TO BRING REDEMPTION IN MESSIAH

A RECORD OF THE GENEALOGY OF JESUS CHRIST [OR MESSIAH] THE SON OF DAVID, THE SON OF ABRAHAM:

MATTHEW 1:1

One can't get more Jewish than David and Abraham! Ultimately God's gift of salvation came through the Jewish people. The seed of the woman, as promised in Genesis 3:16, was born in a manger. When Jesus said, "Salvation is from the Jews" (John 4:22), He was telling the Samaritan woman at the well that it was through the Jewish people, God's first chosen ones, that the Creator of All was pleased to send salvation to the world. Immediately after He spoke those words to her, she responded, "I know that Messiah … is coming," to which Jesus declared, "I who speak to you am He" (vv. 25-26). Redemption came to the world through the Jewish people in the person of Jesus.

Jesus was born as a Jewish man, and He lived a Jewish life. In fact, it was during the Jewish festival of Passover that He proclaimed Himself the Passover Lamb—the Savior of the world. He was raised from the dead on the Jewish festival of First Fruits. The Holy Spirit was given to the early Jewish believers during the festival of Weeks or Shavuot (also known as Pentecost). Through the giving of the law, the temple worship, and the Jewish festivals, we see Jesus.

One day redemption will return to Jerusalem, for Jesus is going to return there to establish His kingdom. Jesus ministered in Jerusalem, left from Jerusalem, and will return to Jerusalem. The Jewish people are still God's chosen people. However, it is deeply important to understand that they need to be reached with the message of Jesus. We must remember that though chosen, like everyone else they are separated from God apart from Jesus. Like Paul, it must be our "heart's desire … that [Israel] may be saved" (Rom. 10:1).

PRAYER

God of Abraham, Isaac, and Jacob, You came to us in the form of a Jewish man. And salvation truly came to me through the Jewish Messiah. Thank You for bringing me to Yourself through Him. Help my love for the Jewish people to grow deep because You chose to send salvation to me through the Jewish people. In my gratefulness to You, and my indebtedness to them, I ask You to open their eyes today. In Jesus' Name, Amen.

JESUS CAME FOR THE JEWISH PEOPLE

[JESUS] ANSWERED, "I WAS SENT ONLY TO
THE LOST SHEEP OF ISRAEL."

MATTHEW 15:24

Jesus was sent and commissioned to the house of Israel—to them and no one else. Of course, the gospel later was extended to the rest of the world, but in its historical and biblical context, Jesus came for my Jewish people—for one people alone. Yet even today, my people to whom Jesus was commissioned "to seek and to save" (Luke 19:10), remain, for the most part, nationally separated from, and have rejected Jesus as Messiah.

Of course, it is true that Jesus prophesied that only "a few" would find "the road that leads to life" (Matt. 7:14). He also announced privately to His disciples that the prophesy of Isaiah 6:9-10 was being fulfilled in their presence, namely that Israel would hear and observe, but that their hearts would be hardened, lest they should understand and be healed (see Matt. 13:14-15). Even the most dedicated and disciplined of Israel itself—the leaders of the Jewish community—remained stubborn in their resistance to Messiah Jesus despite the powerful miracles and healings performed by Him.

Again, Jesus came for the Jewish people. And, after choosing the twelve men who became His first Jewish followers, we are told, "These twelve Jesus sent out with the following instructions: 'Do not go among the Gentiles or enter any town of the Samaritans. Go rather to the lost sheep of Israel. As you go preach this message. "The kingdom of heaven is near"'" (Matthew 10: 5-7). Amazingly enough, even though the Great Commission directs us to "make disciples of all nations" (Matt. 28:19), beginning in Jerusalem (see Acts 1:8), His instructions to the disciples as they began their ministry was to go only to the Jewish community. His ministry was to Israel. His heart was for His Jewish people. Jesus came for them first.

PRAYER

Lord, help me to see and remember how You came for the Jewish community. Your desire was for them to see Your kingdom first. Please help each of us in Your church to understand Your great love for Israel and for the Jewish people. Help my heart to turn to them as Your heart did. May my prayers go up for the people you came to save. In Your Name, Jesus, Amen.

PAUL'S HEART FOR HIS PEOPLE

BROTHERS, MY HEART'S DESIRE AND PRAYER TO
GOD FOR THE ISRAELITES IS THAT THEY MAY BE SAVED.
ROMANS 10:1

The apostle Paul came from a very religious Jewish background. Before becoming a believer in Jesus he persecuted Christians, having them put to death. However, God got to Paul's heart. Jesus revealed Himself to him, and his life was changed forever. He became the greatest voice of the truth of Jesus in all of history. In fact, the apostle Paul wrote much of the New Testament.

The apostle Paul was Jewish, and yet he was called by God to be an apostle to the Gentiles. His main ministry was as a church planter in Asia Minor, an area in which he naturally would meet and reach mostly non-Jewish people. Paul spent his time walking the streets, traveling from place to place, proclaiming the message of salvation in Jesus, reaching people for the Lord, making disciples of new believers, and raising up leadership for new churches. He was very successful, and in large part, the church began as a result of the apostle Paul's ministry. And, again, the primary group he was called to reach were Gentiles.

However, Paul's unceasing burden for his kinsmen is evident in his life and ministry as well. It is an area of his ministry that often is overlooked by many, and yet, it is an area that should be understood by the church today. Paul's heart for the Jewish people and the special place they had in his life, is also a reflection of God's love for the Jewish people. The Jews had a special place in Paul's heart, they have a special place in God's heart, and they need to have a special place in our hearts as well.

As we watch Paul's ministry develop through the book of Acts, he makes his love for his Jewish people quite evident. Though called as an apostle to the Gentiles, Paul makes it a point to go to the synagogue first in every city he visited (see Acts 17:2). There, in the synagogue, he would present the truth of Jesus to the Jewish community. He looked for those Jewish people whose hearts were receptive to the message of the Messiah. Paul spent a lot of his time in the synagogue, but once he had proclaimed the message of Jesus to his people, he would then proclaim Messiah to the Gentiles, believing that one day they would take Jesus back to the Jews. Though many, if not most, of his kinsmen often rejected him, Paul did not give up on them. Neither does God.

PRAYER

God of Abraham, Isaac, and Jacob, You do not give up on those whom You love. I believe that Your Holy Spirit is at work in the lives of many Jewish people because You love them so dearly. I thank You for Your love for Israel and the Jewish community. As the apostle Paul prayed, I pray, that my "heart's desire and prayer" for Israel "is that they may be saved." Please make it happen, even today. In Your mighty Name, Amen.

TO THE JEW FIRST

FOR I AM NOT ASHAMED OF THE GOSPEL,
FOR IT IS THE POWER OF GOD FOR SALVATION
TO EVERYONE WHO BELIEVES,
TO THE JEW FIRST AND ALSO TO THE GREEK
[OR GENTILE].
ROMANS 1:16, ESV

When Paul wrote his letter to the church in Rome, thirty years after the crucifixion, death, and resurrection of Jesus, a problem had developed in the church. Because of the diligent work of those first Jewish missionaries—Peter, Paul, Barnabas, Silas, and others—the church had grown significantly. It had also become primarily Gentile.

Unfortunately, some in the church were beginning to look unfavorably upon the Jewish community. People began to forget the importance of the Jewish people in God's heart and plan. Some were even saying that God had rejected the Jewish people! Paul surely remembered Jesus' instructions to the disciples, "Do not go among the Gentiles or enter any town of the Samaritans. Go rather to the lost sheep of Israel" (Matt. 10:5-6). He knew that Jesus sent the disciples out, first to Jerusalem (to the Jewish people), then "Judea and Samaria, and [finally] to the ends of the earth" (Acts 1:8).

Paul had a burning desire in his heart to see his Jewish people come to know the Messiah. Paul remembered that Jesus wept over Jerusalem, for Jesus' heart broke for those in the Jewish community who were rejecting Him. Paul's heart was broken too. He began his letter to the church in Rome by proclaiming the salvation message, saying, "I am not ashamed of the gospel, for it is the power of God for salvation to everyone who believes, to the Jew first and also to the Greek [or Gentile]." Some theologians even have said that this verse is more correctly translated: "to the Jew especially, and also to the Gentile."

Then in chapters 9-11 of Romans, Paul comes to the pinnacle of his letter. He had already established and penned some of the most foundational doctrines of the faith, but now he turns his attention to the Jewish community and his burden for them. He wanted the church to know how important the Jewish people are. In Romans 9:3, Paul states, in essence, that he would be willing to give up his salvation and spend eternity separated from God for the sake of the Jewish people. I am sure there were many in the church in Rome thinking, "Who cares about the Jews? God has rejected them. They killed Jesus. They aren't important to God anymore." But Paul was a great example of a missionary to the Gentiles who went to the Jewish people first. Though called primarily to those who were not of Jewish decent, he always stopped to proclaim the message of Jesus at the synagogue first. The apostle Paul was a living example of: "To the Jew first."

PRAYER

Help me always to remember, "to the Jew first," in my heart, in my prayers, in my giving. Thank You for the Jewish people. Open their eyes, and the eyes of all nations to Your truth. In Jesus' Name, Amen.

✡

ISRAEL—NOT REJECTED

GOD DID NOT REJECT HIS PEOPLE, WHOM HE FOREKNEW.
ROMANS 1 1:2

In Romans 10:1, Paul expresses the pain in his heart for the Jewish community and his "heart's desire … that they may be saved." He knew that God was not giving up on the Jewish people. He was not going to give up on them either—not by a long shot! Then in Romans 11:1, Paul asks, "Did God reject his people?" And a few verses later, he continues, "Again I ask: Did they stumble so as to fall beyond recovery?" (Rom. 11:11). It only stands to reason that there were those in the church in Rome who were saying that God had rejected the Jewish people and that they had fallen "beyond recovery." They were saying that the Jewish people had been "punted" by God—that they were no longer important, and that God did not care about them. But Paul corrects that misunderstanding by saying that not only has God not rejected the Jewish people, but also that "salvation has come to the Gentiles" in order "to provoke [Israel] to jealousy"! (Rom. 11:11, NIV; followed by KJV).

There is only one group of people in all of Scripture, mentioned by God by name, about whom He says, in essence, "Church, in your efforts to reach the world with the message of grace and salvation in Jesus, I want you to know, there is one group of people who has a special place in My heart. There is one group who has a special place in My plan. There is one group of people to whom you are indebted. And, if it not for this group of people, you would not have the church, you would not have the cross, you would not have the Lord's Supper, you would not have the Bible, you would not have Jesus, you would not have salvation. Don't forget the Jewish people!"

If there has been one group of people almost completely neglected by the church for the past 2000 years it has been my Jewish people. Some have called the Jewish people "the great omission of the Great Commission." Paul knew the importance of the Jewish people. In fact, Paul says something in Romans 11 that is very telling: "I magnify my ministry [to the Gentiles] in order somehow to make my fellow Jews jealous, and thus save some of them" (Rom. 11:13-14, ESV). Paul saw his ministry to the Gentiles as a means to get the gospel back to the Jewish community! Paul knew. We need to know as well.

PRAYER

Give me the heart of Jesus and the apostle Paul for the Jewish community. Help me to more deeply and fully understand the church's responsibility to take the message of Messiah Jesus back to the people who gave us Jesus. Thank You for them. In Messiah's Name, Amen.

✡

THE LETTER OF THE LAW

FOR WHAT THE LAW WAS POWERLESS TO DO IN THAT
IT WAS WEAKENED BY SINFUL NATURE,
GOD DID BY SENDING HIS OWN SON IN THE LIKENESS
OF SINFUL MAN TO BE A SIN OFFERING.

ROMANS 8:3

According to the Scriptures, when Moses came down from Mt. Sinai he was carrying two tablets of the law, with each having five commandments inscribed on it, for a total of ten. Those Ten Commandments, found in Exodus 20:1-17, were not all the laws, but represented the foundation for the others. Moses went on to pen the rest of the Law in the Torah (*Torah* means *law*), which finally totaled 613 commandments. Of these, 365 commandments are negative commandments, instructing the Israelites what *not to do*. The remaining 248 are positive commandments, instructing the Israelites what *to do*.

From the beginning of the giving of the law, its weight became too difficult to bear. The law was impossible to keep in total perfection, so the Lord added within the law a provision for the atonement of sin. That provision was the sacrificial system performed by the priests in the tabernacle and the temple. Yet even with this provision it was impossible for the Torah to be followed perfectly. But why would God give us laws that were impossible to follow?

The Bible says, in essence, that is was the Lord's way of showing us

51

our need for Him. The Law reveals our need for faith and obedience, because "man looks at the outward appearance, but the LORD looks at the heart" (1 Sam. 16:7). Today, Jewish people who do not yet know Jesus strive to follow the Torah, for like every other religion, rabbinical Judaism emphasizes adherence to the Law for entrance into heaven.

However, God, knowing we could never satisfy the letter of the Law, made this promise through the prophet Jeremiah: "'This is the covenant I will make with the house of Israel after that time,' declares the LORD. 'I will put my law in their minds and write it on their hearts. I will be their God, and they will be my people. No longer will a man teach his neighbor, or a man his brother, saying "Know the LORD," because they will all know me…. For I will forgive their wickedness and will remember their sins no more'" (Jer. 31:33-34).

Jesus ushered in the new covenant, and bore the penalty of the Law on Himself on the cross. Thus, by faith the fullness of the Law lives in all who believe.

PRAYER

Dear Lord, I thank You for loving me and for allowing me to come into Your presence on the basis of faith. Thank You that You gave us the new covenant, and yet, that the Law remains to help us understand how separated we are from You apart from Your hand of mercy. Please open the eyes of the Jewish people who attempt to follow Your Torah perfectly. Help those who are depending on their own righteousness to accept Your gift of mercy and forgiveness in Jesus. In His Name, Amen.

THE WHOLE OF THE LAW

DO NOT THINK THAT I HAVE COME TO ABOLISH
THE LAW OR THE PROPHETS; I HAVE NOT COME TO
ABOLISH THEM, BUT TO FULFILL THEM.
MATTHEW 5:1 7

Jesus sat down on a mountainside and began to teach His disciples—a Jewish rabbi, teaching His Jewish students. But the multitudes began to gather and listen as well, as rabbi Jesus began to expound on the Law.

The Jewish Scriptures are split naturally into three sections, known in Hebrew as the Torah, Nevi'im, and Ketuv'im. Religious Jews call the Jewish Bible the Tanak, which is actually an acronym comprised from these same three sections: the Torah, Nevi'im, and Ketuv'im. In English, these divisions are known as the Law, the Prophets, and the Writings. The Torah is the first five books of the Old Testament: Genesis, Exodus, Leviticus, Numbers, and Deuteronomy; the Prophets comprise all the Old Testament prophetic books; while the Writings are the historical and poetic writings such as Psalms, Proverbs, Song of Solomon, Lamentations, and Kings, etc. The Jewish Bible in its entirety is what Christians refer to as the Old Testament.

Jesus recognized all three sections of the Jewish Scriptures and taught through them. He did not have a New Testament—He was living it! And when He taught the Jewish people who gathered on the mountainside, He explained to them that He was the fulfillment of the Law and the

Prophets. He had come to give us a greater law—one that encapsulated all the Old Testament law and more—and had come in fulfillment of the Prophets, each of whom looked forward to the Messiah who would redeem humanity from bondage to sin and death.

Messiah Jesus made it known that our righteousness must exceed the righteousness of the Pharisees. He taught, for example, that adultery is more than having an affair with a woman, but also is lusting in one's heart; that murder is more than killing someone, for we murder by using angry, rage-filled words against another person. God told us through the Jewish prophets we could not reach this righteous standard. But Jesus, the Jewish Messiah, took our sin upon Himself that we might enter into a relationship with the Father by faith in Him—His resurrected Son!

PRAYER

God of the Word, thank You for helping me understand who You are through Your revealed Word—Jesus. As a rabbi, He taught me and helped me understand that my righteousness is not enough, even if it exceeded that of the most religious—that "all [my] righteous acts are like filthy rags" (Isa. 64:6). Thank You for loving me, for sending Your Son to die for me, and for helping me to know You through Messiah Jesus. In His Name, Amen.

THE FIRST COMMANDMENT

BE FRUITFUL AND INCREASE IN NUMBER.
GENESIS 1:22

Did you know there are 613 commandments in the Old Testament, the first being "Be fruitful and increase in number"? God gave this first commandment so Adam and Eve would fill the earth with offspring. Yet this was followed by 612 more. And the Jewish Rabbis added even more commandments. These rabbinical laws were added in order to prevent the Jewish people from breaking the biblical law. This is known as "fencing in the law."

Many know that orthodox Jewish people do not drive on the Sabbath, but erroneously think this is because God told the Israelites not to work on that day. The real reason, however, is that the turning of the car key creates a spark, which the rabbis equate with starting a fire—something forbidden by the law on the Sabbath. Therefore, orthodox Jews do not drive, cook, or even turn on lights during the Sabbath day.

Many of these laws, however, are not in the Bible, but have been passed down by the rabbis over the millennia to "protect" the Jewish community from breaking the law. Yet in the process, they have placed an undue burden, or yoke, on those who follow their religion. The reason Jesus came was so that yoke would be made easier (see Matt. 11:30). He came to carry our burden, and "to proclaim freedom for the captives" (Isa. 61:1). May our prayer be that the Jewish community would accept His "burden [that] is light" (Matt. 11:30), which Jesus—

Yeshua—came to bring.

PRAYER

Dear Lord, I thank You for the freedom You have given me in Messiah Jesus. He came to set me free, and when I am in Him, I am "free indeed"! (John 8:36). His yoke is not heavy—His "burden is light." Help me always remember that He came to remove the burden of the law—that in Him I am free. And I pray that You would open the eyes of the Jewish people—that they would be free as well. May the people of Israel come to know the grace Jesus came to bring. In Jesus' name, Amen.

LOVING ISRAEL THE BIBLICAL WAY

YOU WHO BRING GOOD TIDINGS TO ZION, GO UP
ON A HIGH MOUNTAIN. YOU WHO BRING GOOD
TIDINGS TO JERUSALEM, LIFT UP YOUR VOICE WITH
A SHOUT, LIFT IT UP, DO NOT BE AFRAID; SAY TO THE
TOWNS OF JUDAH, "HERE IS YOUR GOD!"

ISAIAH 40:9

Israel—its land and its people—is one of the smallest countries of the world, and yet it is in the news every day. The name *Israel* is used nearly 2000 times in the Bible, while *Jerusalem* is mentioned 760 times. The world has its eyes focused on Israel. Some love her. Some hate her. Israel—the Jewish homeland.

It is very popular in evangelical Christian circles to communicate one's love for Israel and the Jewish community. Pastors and Christian groups jump on the "love Israel" bandwagon. Loving Israel is important, but it cannot come at the expense of the proclamation of the gospel to Israel. Too often we substitute what feels good for what is right. We gravitate toward what is accepted rather than toward what is commanded.

There is a danger in loving Israel if we are misguided, misdirected, or don't understand what truly loving Israel and the Jewish people means. Building bridges of understanding often comes with strings attached.

Most Christians focus more on loving the Jewish people and Israel, while neglecting to communicate the gospel to the Jewish people.

It is much easier to show love and friendship, because it feels good. It is applauded. Telling someone they need Jesus and are risking eternal separation from God if they do not consider His claims is difficult, uncomfortable, and frightening to do. Therefore, individuals and groups often placate their own feelings by substituting their kind of love for the kind of love we are commanded to show.

Remember—we are commanded to take the Good News of Messiah Jesus to everyone. We are not given another option. Everyone needs to hear, but do not forget: "to the Jew first" (Rom. 1:16, ESV).

PRAYER

Lord, help me to love others by showing them Your truth. I know that to truly show our love, I must lay aside my fears and my insecurities to share Your Good News. Please help me to look for opportunities and please open doors into the lives of those I love who do not yet know You. Help me to do what is right, not expedient. You showed Your love for Israel by giving Your life for them. Help me to take that message to them. In Messiah's Name. Amen.

GIVING TO ISRAEL THE BIBLICAL WAY

I WILL BLESS THOSE WHO BLESS YOU.

GENESIS 12:3

Not only are we commanded to pray for the Jewish people, but also we are given instruction to share our material blessings with the Jewish community. The apostle Paul had been to Macedonia and Achaia where he received a love offering for "the saints in Jerusalem" (Rom. 15:26). These saints primarily consisted of Jewish people who had accepted the Lord and were a part of the church in Jerusalem. Though the offering that he had taken was going to Jewish believers in Jesus, the principle of giving to the needs of any Jewish person is made clear.

Paul wrote, "Macedonia and Achaia were pleased to make a contribution for the poor among the saints in Jerusalem. They were pleased to do it, and indeed they owe it to them. For if the Gentiles have shared in the Jews' spiritual blessings, they owe it to the Jews to share with them their material blessings." Romans 15:26-27

The church has received many blessings from the Jewish people. They gave us the Bible, and it is through Jesus—the Jewish Messiah— that God brought salvation to the world. The very first missionaries were Jewish. The sacred acts of communion and baptism come from

Jewish traditions. The church began as a Jewish movement. The Jews have blessed us beyond comprehension with "spiritual blessings." We owe it to them, according to Scripture, to share our "material blessings."

There are many ways to share blessings with the Jewish people. There are Jews in need around the world, and there are special ministries devoted to helping them. However, if you support a ministry doing benevolent work among the Jewish people, please make sure they are a Christian ministry and believe in sharing the gospel as well. If you have a Jewish friend, whether they are in material need or not, look for opportunities to bless them. Birthday? Anniversary? Special holiday? When they ask why you are reaching out, tell them because you have received many great gifts from their community. Tell them, in fact, that if it were not for the Jewish people, you would not have Jesus.

PRAYER

Dear Lord, Messiah came through the Jewish people and ministered in Israel. Please bless and protect them. I ask that You would help me to know how I can help them in a material way. I pray for the poor among them in Israel and around the world. I thank You that through them You have given me so much. Help me to know how to give back. In Your Name, Amen.

LOVING ISRAEL IN THE GREATEST WAY

HOW, THEN, CAN THEY CALL ON THE ONE THEY HAVE
NOT BELIEVED IN? AND HOW CAN THEY BELIEVE IN THE
ONE OF WHOM THEY HAVE NOT HEARD? AND HOW CAN
THEY HEAR WITHOUT SOMEONE PREACHING TO THEM?

ROMANS 10:14

The greatest way we can show love for Israel and the Jewish community is by sharing the message of Jesus with them. He is the greatest gift they gave us, and it is our responsibility to take Jesus back to them.

Unfortunately this command has been, and continues to be, sorely neglected by the church. Church history is littered with instances of Jewish people being persecuted in the name of Jesus, rather than being wooed to the One who wept over Jerusalem and loved His people so much. It is much easier to "pray for the peace of Jerusalem" (Ps. 122:6), than it is to proclaim the "Prince of Peace" (Isa. 9:6) to Jerusalem. It is much easier to share material blessings with Jewish people, thinking that material blessings will suffice, than it is to share the gift of the gospel—the blessing of knowing Messiah Jesus personally.

Yet the apostle Paul's heart was broken when he said, "I speak the truth in Christ—I am not lying, my conscience confirms it in the Holy

Spirit—I have great sorrow and unceasing anguish in my heart. For I could wish that I myself were cursed and cut off from Christ for the sake of my brothers, those of my own race, the people of Israel" (Rom. 9:1-4). Paul's heart was for his Jewish people first, and Jesus Himself wept over Jerusalem and sent his disciples out beginning in Jerusalem because of the enormous responsibility to take the gospel to the Jewish community.

The Jewish people and Israel need our prayers, our blessings, and most importantly, our Jesus. The Bible commands us to give them all three. However, without sharing Jesus with them, ultimately our prayers for their peace and our gifts of love will be meaningless. In the end, it is only the gift of Jesus that will bring lasting joy and peace into their lives.

PRAYER

God of Abraham, Isaac, and Jacob, please open Jewish hearts and minds to Jesus today. I ask that the church would rise up and take the message of Messiah back to the special people through whom He came. Please give the church a passion to take Him to the Jewish people in Israel and around the world. May my heart be broken over those whom He loved so much. In Your Name, Amen.

PROPHECY OF BLINDNESS FULFILLED

THIS WAS TO FULFILL THE WORD OF ISAIAH
THE PROPHET: "LORD, WHO HAS BELIEVED OUR
MESSAGE AND TO WHOM HAS THE ARM OF THE
LORD BEEN REVEALED?"
JOHN 12:38

Isaiah saw the glory of God. He knew that one day, the Anointed One, the Messiah, would come to redeem the Jewish people and the world from slavery and bondage to sin. Isaiah spoke of Messiah's birth in Isaiah 7:14, and later spoke of His death and resurrection in Isaiah 53. He prophesied that the Jewish community would, for the most part, reject their Messiah. It was prophesied that they would turn their back on the One who came to save them and bring them peace. Just as the community of ancient Israel scorned the prophets, many would scorn the Messiah. And He continues to be scorned today. Do not most Jews reject Jesus?

Jesus wept over Jerusalem. He wept because it was His desire to gather the Jewish people together under His wings of salvation, and yet at the same time He knew they would not come. He lamented, "O Jerusalem, Jerusalem, you who kill the prophets and stone those sent to you, how often I have longed to gather your children together, as a hen gathers her chicks under her wings, but you were not willing" (Matt. 23:37). Though it was prophesied that the Jewish community would turn their back on Jesus, He never turned His back on them. He had unceasing anguish and pain in His heart over His Jewish brethren.

To this day, most in the Jewish community still do not acknowledge Jesus as Messiah. The religious Jewish person is still waiting for Him to come. But Messiah has already come. Yet the Jewish community is but a microcosm of the rest of humanity. They are lost and separated from God because of sin (see Isaiah 59:2), and are in need of a savior. Though it was prophesied the Jewish people would reject their Messiah Jesus, we need to have the heart of Jesus—one filled with anguish over those who have rejected Him, but who so desperately need to hear. We need to remember that everyone, both Jew and Gentile, need to come to Jesus in order to be in relationship with the God of Abraham, Isaac, and Jacob.

PRAYER

Jesus, You wept over Jerusalem and had unceasing anguish over their rejection of You. Yet most still reject You today. The world is in great need of You, so break and burden my heart today, and give me Your heart for those who do not yet know You. Cause me to shed tears, as You did, over Jerusalem. I earnestly pray that those who do not yet know You will be gathered under Your wings of salvation. In Your Name, Amen.

SALVATION FOR THE GENTILES

I WILL PLANT FOR HER MYSELF IN THE LAND;
I WILL SHOW MY LOVE TO THE ONE I CALLED
"NOT MY LOVED ONE." I WILL SAY TO THOSE CALLED
"NOT MY PEOPLE," "YOU ARE MY PEOPLE;" AND
THEY WILL SAY, "YOU ARE MY GOD."

HOSEA 2:23

To whom is God referring to when He says, "Not my people"? Maybe you—that is, if you are not Jewish. Paul at the very least implies this when he quotes Hosea in Romans 9:25. God spoke through the prophet Hosea explaining that one day the message of salvation would be extended to those who were not initially called the people of God. Through the prophet Isaiah God reiterates the idea of salvation being extended from the Jewish people to the Gentiles, when He says, "I, the LORD, have called you in righteousness; I will take hold of your hand. I will keep you and make you to be a covenant for the people and a light for the Gentiles, to open eyes that are blind, to free the captives from prison and to release from the dungeon those who sit in darkness" (Isa. 42:6-7).

The early Christians, who were all Jewish, did not understand this idea at first. They thought a Gentile who accepted Jesus, the Jewish Messiah, had to convert to Judaism. Two thousand years ago they weren't asking how one could be Jewish and believe in Jesus. They wondered how one could be Gentile and accept Jesus, without first becoming Jewish. Until that point in history everyone who became a believer in the God of Abraham, Isaac, and Jacob became what the Bible calls a proselyte, or a convert to Judaism. But God made it clear through a vision to Peter in Acts 10 that it was possible for Gentiles to accept Jesus without first converting to Judaism. The Gentiles, those who were not the people of God, were accepted by grace, and became partakers of the great covenant of salvation through the Jewish Messiah.

God, in His amazing plan of redemption, brought His truth to the world through the Jewish people—the Israelite community—and then extended His plan of redemption to the Gentiles. And the continuation of that plan of redemption is for the Gentiles to take the message of the Messiah back to the Jewish people!

PRAYER

God of the Jewish people, thank You for accepting me and placing me into Your kingdom by grace through faith. Thank You that I am grafted into the faith of Abraham, and that Your acceptance is not based upon my background, or on my personal heritage, but on Your great and abounding love. Thank You that I am an heir to the throne along with all believers in Jesus, whether Jewish or Gentile by birth. Thank You for accepting me, and I pray that even today You would open the hearts of those who do not yet know You, to Your amazing grace. In Your Name, Amen.

PURPOSE IN ISRAEL'S BLINDNESS

FOR THIS REASON THEY COULD NOT BELIEVE,
BECAUSE, AS ISAIAH SAYS ELSEWHERE:
"HE HAS BLINDED THEIR EYES AND DEADENED THEIR
HEARTS, SO THEY CAN NEITHER SEE WITH THEIR EYES,
NOR UNDERSTAND WITH THEIR HEARTS, NOR TURN—
AND I WOULD HEAL THEM."
JOHN 12:39-40

God gave the Jewish people a temporary blindness for a reason. The truth of God had been given to them first, but God's intent was for it to be extended to Gentiles as well. The blindness of the Jewish community allowed for the inclusion of the Gentiles into the kingdom through faith in Jesus, the Jewish Messiah.

"Because of [Israel's] transgression, salvation has come to the Gentiles to make Israel envious. But if their transgression means riches for the world, and their loss means riches for the Gentiles, how much greater riches will their fullness bring!" (Rom. 11:11-12).

God, in His unsearchable wisdom, gave the Jewish people over to a spiritual blindness in order to include Gentiles in His kingdom. Their blindness came as a result of their transgression. Their community wide failure resulted in the extension of His truth to the surrounding nations through Jesus. It was, and now is, His desire that Gentile believers in Jesus would take the message of Messiah back to the Jewish people from whom it came. "To the Jew first" (Rom. 1:16, ESV), then to the Gentile, and back to the Jewish people!

The spiritual blindness God placed on the Jewish people was not, and is not, a blindness that is terminal. It can be healed. Their eyes can be opened. And, though the Jewish people are "blind" as a community, individual Jewish people have been coming to faith in Messiah Jesus since the first day of His ministry. Blindness "in part" (Rom. 11:25) has come upon Israel, but God has His remnant among them. He is able to remove the scales from their eyes and to open their hearts.

PRAYER

God of Israel, I know that apart from Your grace and the power of Your Holy Spirit no one can truly see Jesus. Help me to see the spiritually blind person today. Give me wisdom to know how to pray for them, and what to say to them. Help me to know how I might be used by You in the lives of others today—that they might see You through me. Thank You for Your love and for using even me—a broken vessel. In Messiah's Name, Amen.

LIVING UNASHAMED

I AM NOT ASHAMED OF THE GOSPEL, BECAUSE IT IS THE POWER OF GOD FOR THE SALVATION OF EVERYONE WHO BELIEVES: FIRST FOR THE JEW, THEN FOR THE GENTILE.

ROMANS 1:16

The apostle Paul began his letter to the church in Rome with this bold statement. Yet often, we focus on the words: "It is the power of God for the salvation of everyone who believes," while ignoring: "First for the Jew."

The word *first*, shows Paul's priority. He was not only saying the gospel first came to the Jewish people, but also that there is a historical priority for them. This priority, however, does not mean exclusivity, but simply means we should never forget that the Jewish people have a special place in God's heart and plan. Just as they had a special place in Jesus' heart, we see from this verse that they were special to Paul. Thus, it stands to reason, that the Jewish people should have a special place in our hearts as well.

Loving the Jewish people is consistent with the very nature of God, just as He proclaimed through Jeremiah: "This is what the LORD says, he who appoints the sun to shine by day, who decrees the moon and stars to shine by night, who stirs up the sea so that its waves roar.... 'Only if these decrees vanish from my sight ... will the descendants of Israel ever cease to be a nation before me'" (Jer. 31:35-36). Of course, the decrees of God regarding nature will never cease to exist until His eternal kingdom is established. The sun still shines, the moon and the stars still cast their glow at night, and the waves still roar in the oceans. And so, the descendants of Israel will exist as a nation as well. Therefore, just as the Lord promised His love to Israel and the Jewish people, we should remember: "First for the Jew."

PRAYER

Dear Lord, I thank You for the uniqueness of Israel. I thank You that the Jewish people have a special place in Your heart and plan. Your faithfulness to Israel shows Your faithfulness to humanity— even me! Thank You that You chose a specific group of people through whom to reveal to me a picture of Your covenantal love. Help me to always lift up the Jewish people and Israel. Give me a heart for the land and the people for whom You care so much. I thank You for them, but most of all I thank You for Your faithfulness and love. In Messiah's Name I pray, Amen.

ISRAEL—A LAND THAT WILL FLOURISH AND PROSPER

IN DAYS TO COME JACOB WILL TAKE ROOT,
ISRAEL WILL BUD AND BLOOM AND FILL ALL
THE WORLD WITH FRUIT.

ISAIAH 2 7:6

International criticism of Israel is certainly increasing. Whether Israel is condemned for protecting herself or for treating its Arab citizens unfairly, the international condemnation of Israel is at an all time high. Israel typically loses the media wars, is scorned by the United Nations, and is hated by the nations surrounding her. Help does not come when they are attacked, but condemnation is quick when they retaliate. As the world's animosity grows, the battle rages in and around the land of Israel.

Of course, this is nothing new. Amazingly the tiny nation of Israel, slightly smaller than the state New Jersey, attracts the attention of the world. Since its establishment in 1948 after the Nazi Holocaust of World War II, it has been attacked, condemned, criticized, and scorned by nation after nation. The biblical truth is that Israel and the Jewish people have been, and will always be, the target of the world's ridicule. Few people or countries come to the aid of Israel, while many gather against her. But God has a plan for Israel and for the Jewish people.

One of the plans for Israel was that, despite surrounding opposition and criticism, it would grow and be a testimony to the goodness of God. Since its establishment in 1948, Israel—a desert for the most part—has bloomed. Though the prophecy has not yet come to complete fulfillment, Isaiah speaks of a day when: "The desert and the parched land will be glad; the wilderness will rejoice and blossom" (Isa. 35:1). When Israel became a nation, her people immediately began irrigating the deserts, and as a result, the nation has become a major agricultural producer, exporting her products to Europe and beyond. Just as today's text prophesized, "Israel will … fill all the world with fruit."

Because God chose the Jewish people through whom to bring us salvation in the person of Messiah Jesus, He promises to bless Israel. Those promises include protection as a people, and prosperity as a nation. Out of Israel and through the Jewish people has come, and will continue to come, some of the major medical, technological, scientific, agricultural, and economic advances known to humankind. This reality is a function of God's promises, as well as the Jewish community's resolve, to always strive for that which is excellent to advance society.

PRAYER

Thank You, God of Abundance, for blessing the land and the people of Israel. Continue to bring from Israel advances for the entire world. Make Your glory known to them and through them. May Your glory be known to all. We thank You for the gifts we have received from Israel, especially the greatest gift of all—our Savior. In His Name, Amen.

ISRAEL—AN OPEN LAND

ARISE, SHINE, FOR YOUR LIGHT HAS COME, AND
THE GLORY OF THE LORD RISES UPON YOU.

ISAIAH 60:1

There is only one democracy in the Middle East—Israel. Thus, there is only one hope for freedom in that area of the world, and again, it is Israel. Because Israel is a free democracy, the proclamation of the gospel there is legal and we can thank God that there are missionaries throughout Israel reaching out to both the Jewish and Muslim communities.

Yet there is opposition to the proclamation of the gospel in Israel, but typically it does not come from the secular Jewish community. Though most Israelis are open to the message of Jesus, the greatest opposition comes from those who are religious, and at times, there is great hostility—even to the point of violence. However, usually the police are there to make sure no one is harmed, and that the freedom of speech is protected. We should thank God that Israel is a land where one can preach the message of Jesus in freedom.

Not only is Israel an open country to proclaim the message of Jesus but also there are many Jewish people in Israel open to His truth. During my own ministries' times of outreach in Israel, it is not uncommon for us to get the names of hundreds of Jewish people who are interested in exploring the reality of Jesus in more depth. Often they are quite open to sharing their thoughts, or to receiving more information—even a

New Testament! In essence, the Jewish people in Israel are becoming more and more open to the message of Jesus.

Although we have not yet come to the great day of ingathering of the Jewish community to Messiah Jesus, or to the time when Israel is brought together as a nation under His wings, the day is hastening. And, as it nears, the work of God among the Jewish people is increasing, and will continue to increase. Praise God for what He is doing now in Israel and for what is yet to come!

PRAYER

Dear God of Israel, thank You for making the nation of Israel democratic and free. Thank You that the gospel of Jesus can be proclaimed in the land. Help those taking the message to be faithful and strong. Help those who hear to believe and receive. May Your truth go forth in the land of Israel and to the Jewish community worldwide. In Messiah Jesus' Name, Amen.

ISRAEL'S NEED OF THE GOSPEL

HOW BEAUTIFUL ON THE MOUNTAINS ARE THE FEET OF THOSE WHO BRING GOOD NEWS, WHO PROCLAIM PEACE, WHO BRING GOOD TIDINGS, WHO PROCLAIM SALVATION, WHO SAY TO ZION, "YOUR GOD REIGNS."

ISAIAH 52:7

Jesus wept over Jerusalem. He looked over the city and lamented, "O Jerusalem, Jerusalem, you who kill the prophets and stone those sent to you, how often I have longed to gather your children together, as a hen gathers her chicks under her wings, but you were not willing" (Matt. 23:37). Earlier, He had sent His disciples out with these instructions, "Do not go among the Gentiles or enter any town of the Samaritans. Go rather to the lost sheep of Israel. As you go preach this message: 'The kingdom of heaven is near'" (Matt. 10:5-7). Israel and Jerusalem have a special place in God's heart. Though my people have historically "not [been] willing," God's love for them is still the same. He loved them so much that he sent Messiah redeemer to become their salvation.

Today, though some are still "not willing" to hear the message, many are. And it is our obligation to sow the seed, proclaim the message, and take the Good News to Israel, with the hope of a great harvest and impact for the kingdom of God. Many believers are there now—sharing the gospel. There are missionaries and messianic congregations throughout the land of Israel, proclaiming the Good News of Messiah Jesus. Tracts are being distributed, banners are being raised, and conversations are taking place. The Word of God is going forth in Israel to the Jewish people.

As the world continues to focus on events in the Middle East and Israel, we must be there. As the world looks at Israel with scorn, we must be there. As Israel waits in fear, wondering when the next attack is going to come, we must be there. As we wait for the Messiah to return to bring His peace, we must be there.

PRAYER

Abba, Father, Your children in Your land need to hear about Your love for them in Messiah. I ask that your faithful workers in Israel will shout it from the rooftops (see Matt. 10:27). Please send even more workers. And please use them to "bring good tidings" and "proclaim salvation." And cause Israel to hear, "Messiah Jesus, reigns!" In His Holy Name, Amen.

ONLY MESSIAH JESUS

SALVATION IS FOUND IN NO ONE ELSE, FOR THERE IS NO OTHER NAME UNDER HEAVEN … BY WHICH WE MUST BE SAVED.

ACTS 4:1 2

With the possible exception of Luke, the writers of the New Testament were Jewish. They wrote the New Testament from a Jewish perspective, and although it may sound strange to say, they didn't have the New Testament as a reference. Yet most Christians often overlook this logical fact. The New Testament is comprised of Jewish books, written by Jewish people, within a Jewish context, about the Jewish Messiah—Jesus.

There are two important statements communicated in the New Testament regarding the truth of Jesus, especially when it comes to attempting to understand His message in its Jewish context. The first is John 14:6, where Messiah Jesus says, "I am the way and the truth and the life. No one comes to the Father except through me." The second is today's text verse, where Peter utters the same basic truth, "Salvation is found in no one else, for there is no other name under heaven … by which we must be saved."

While many in the church today are aware of these statements of Jesus and Peter, most do not consider their contexts. In John 14:6, Jesus is proclaiming Himself as the only way to the Father during the Last

Supper. He and his disciples were sitting around the Passover table, alone in an upper room of a home in Jerusalem. There were no Gentiles there to hear Jesus proclaim Himself the Messiah and the only way to the Father. His audience was the disciples, and they were all Jewish.

Peter, proclaiming the same message in Acts, was speaking to the Sanhedrin, the Jewish supreme court of his day. Assuredly, there were no non-Jewish people in the presence of a special convening of the Jewish Supreme Court 2000 years ago!

And he said to them, there is only one way. The way is Jesus!

PRAYER

God, thank You that the message of salvation was given to us through the Jewish people. Thank You that Messiah Jesus came to us in the form of a Jewish man, and that His Good News was sent to them first. Please give the Jews of today "eyes to see ... and ears to hear" (Ezek. 12:2) the message that Messiah has come, and that His Name is Jesus. In His Name, Amen.

MY PEOPLE—A PEOPLE WITHOUT HOPE

COME, LET US RETURN TO THE LORD.
HE HAS TORN US TO PIECES BUT HE WILL
HEAL US; HE HAS INJURED US BUT HE WILL
BIND UP OUR WOUNDS.
HOSEA 6:1

The following quote is from an article entitled "Sin … A Yom Kippur Essay" in the Jewish Journal of Los Angeles. It is by Amy Klein, a Jewish woman and writer (www.KleinsLines. com), whose words echo the thoughts of countless Jewish people who annually attend synagogue on the Day of Atonement.

"Yom Kippurs pass, awesome in their familiarity. ... I am repentant at times and questioning at others. 'For the sin we have sinned before you through denial and false promises….' This is the one (confession) I have the most trouble with. My false promises. Yes, I know in the three steps of repentance—acknowledgement of the sin, regret for the sin, and a promise not to do the sin again—I am clear on the first two. But year after year, I find myself in schul (synagogue), making the same promises, having the same regrets, seeing the same failures—with new ones added to boot. And I grow weary. Wary. How could I be here every year saying the same things, knowing I wouldn't manage to keep my word? How meaningless is that? It is like a Hollywood marriage—they say the vows, but everyone knows it will never last. All my life I worried so about my sins, my wrongdoings, my faults, my failures, that the only image I had was of a vengeful, exacting God towering above us mercilessly. I recently returned to services. Maybe my sins—whatever they are, however and whoever is counting—are forgiven. Maybe."

Without knowing God, any such hope is fleeting at best. Humanity is separated from God because of sin. My people are no different. Striving to please God in our own power gets us nowhere because we are powerless against sin. And so my people strive, humanity strives, hoping but never knowing, praying and always wondering, striving for a relationship with God that only Jesus can give.

PRAYER

God of Hope, give hope to those who do not yet know You. Thank You for giving me hope in the Messiah of Israel who suffered on a cross and died to carry the sins that I am unable to carry. Thank You for being my kipporah, my covering. As Jews and others around the world strive and hope for You, help them to see Your salvation. Let them understand and receive your forgiveness today. In Messiah's Name, Amen.

MY PEOPLE—A PEOPLE WITHOUT SPIRITUAL DIRECTION

"FOR THE LIPS OF A PRIEST OUGHT TO PRESERVE
KNOWLEDGE, AND FROM HIS MOUTH MEN SHOULD
SEEK INSTRUCTION—BECAUSE HE IS THE MESSENGER
OF THE LORD ALMIGHTY. BUT YOU HAVE TURNED
FROM THE WAY AND BY YOUR TEACHING HAVE CAUSED
MANY TO STUMBLE; YOU HAVE VIOLATED
THE COVENANT WITH LEVI," SAYS THE
LORD ALMIGHTY.
MALACHI 2:7-8

Some have called the Jewish people a missionary people without a mission. In the Old Testament, my people were called to be those who carried the truth of the one true God to the rest of the world. The priests were to lead them and give them direction. Yet even they failed in their mission to their own people—something God knew would happen. Though chosen by God, my people failed; we dropped the ball. But God never fails. He promised Messiah would carry the burden of the law for everyone, that through faith in Him we could enter into a relationship with the Holy One of Israel. "Because of their transgression, salvation has come to the [world] (Rom. 11:11).

My people have, as a community, rejected God's provision in Messiah Jesus. Just as my priests came to God with unworthy sacrifices, so today if we come to God on our own merits, we come empty-handed and unworthy. Our works, our way, is not God's way. One can only come to God based on the merits of Jesus.

Thus, my people have lost the "mission" mindset. No longer are we a missionary people for God. Instead, we have replaced that God-given mission. Spiritual hope has been replaced by a desire to "make the world a better place in which to live." Today we witness the world being blessed by the humanitarian and philanthropic endeavors of many in the Jewish community. While this is a good thing, what God desires from my people is purposeful living focused on the One who loves them so much, and who died for their sins.

PRAYER

God of Jacob, people around the world, like Jacob, have always wrestled with You. Even the name Israel means "to wrestle with God." My Jewish people have wrestled on their own, substituting what they think to be right for what is truly right. They try as many others do, to substitute their form of "sacrifice" for what you desire. Help them—help the world—see and understand, that we cannot save ourselves. Cause them to turn to You, O Holy One of Israel. In Your Name I pray, Amen.

MY PEOPLE—A PEOPLE WITHOUT GOD

SURELY THE ARM OF THE LORD IS NOT TOO
SHORT TO SAVE, NOR HIS EAR TOO DULL TO HEAR.
BUT YOUR INIQUITIES HAVE SEPARATED YOU FROM
YOUR GOD; YOUR SINS HAVE HIDDEN HIS FACE FROM
YOU, SO THAT HE WILL NOT HEAR.

ISAIAH 59:1-2

Dennis Prager, best-selling Jewish author and radio personality, in a fall 2003 article entitled "Ignoring God" from "Kosher Spirit" magazine, writes: "The people who brought G-d to the world don't have much to do with Him. Perhaps the saddest aspect of modern Jewish life is how unimportant G-d is to most Jews. Reasons for this include Jews identify religion with persecution and secularism with freedom; Jews are the most highly educated ethnic group in America and therefore secularly influenced from kindergarten to graduate school; even religious Jewish life often has little G-d-centeredness. (Please note that Dennis Prager, an Orthodox Jewish man, out of respect for God, does not fully write His name. Instead, he writes G-d.)

"Whatever the reason, it is a fact that G-d plays little role in Jewish life. … It is a tragedy for Jews individually, since without G-d in one's life, one's sense of purpose and level of happiness are dramatically affected. Human beings are wired for the transcendent, and children, in particular, suffer from the absence of G-d in their lives. … That most Jewish parents are unable to say to their child, 'G-d loves you' or 'Look at that gorgeous sunset—isn't G-d amazing?' is sad beyond words.

"Many Jewish parents fear that their child may become 'too religious' but never worry that they might become too secular. … Yet 'too secular' is exactly what most Jews have become, even many who observe some Jewish laws. The average Bar-Mitzvah is devoid of G-d and sanctity; and the average Jewish education, even in many Jewish day schools, may be Hebrew centered or even observance-centered, but it is rarely G-d-centered."

It shocks people when I share the statistic in churches that fewer that 20 percent of Jews are considered religious by Orthodox Jewish standards, and that 70 percent of the Jewish community is not affiliated with a synagogue. Furthermore, most Jewish people in Israel are either atheists or agnostics, meaning they either do not believe in God, or they are not sure He exists. It is a sad fact that my people have, for the most part, abandoned their relationship with God who loves them so much. Jesus looked over the city of Jerusalem and wept as he saw how far my people had strayed from their Maker. My people need to return to God, and Jesus is the way to Him.

PRAYER

Father it is our human tendency to live as if You do not exist. We lean toward following religion rather than pursuing a relationship with You. Although all of us are in need of that relationship, most of us live as if You are nonexistent. The Jewish people need You as we all do. Please open their eyes to Your love. Help them to understand that their Messiah has come and that His name is Jesus. Please bless them with a deep understanding of Your love for them, and Your provision for them in Him. In Messiah's Name I pray, Amen.

MY PEOPLE—A PEOPLE SEARCHING

"YOU WILL SEEK ME AND FIND ME WHEN YOU SEEK ME
WITH ALL YOUR HEART. I WILL BE FOUND BY YOU,"
DECLARES THE LORD, "AND WILL BRING YOU BACK
FROM CAPTIVITY."
JEREMIAH 29:13-14

When Jeremiah wrote these words my people were in captivity—literal captivity. They had been carried into exile from Jerusalem to Babylon. Jerusalem had come under siege, Solomon's temple had been destroyed, and King Nebuchadnezzar had raided the city. Captivity had come due to their disobedience to God. Though warned numerous times of impending exile, my people continued to worship idols and turn their backs on the God who loved them so much. Captivity had been prophesied and captivity came. Their spiritual captivity had turned into literal captivity. Their hearts were hard and they turned away from God, but He said to them, "Seek me with all your heart [and] I will be found by you."

Today Jewish people are searching like never before. Some are searching for the truth and come to Jesus, while others are searching elsewhere, for spiritual searching can lead in many directions. Just as in Jeremiah's day, many of my Jewish people are turning to other gods, not the God of Israel. Some are experimenting in other religions such as Buddhism and Hinduism, and many are dabbling in the occult. The primary reason Jewish people are looking for spiritual satisfaction outside mainstream Judaism is the lack of spiritual substance most experience in the synagogue from their rabbis and from the Jewish community itself.

Yet God has His hand on my people and will continue to draw them to Himself. Though many have fallen away from Him and live in spiritual captivity, God can set them free—the Son can set them free. "So if the Son sets you free, you will be free indeed" (John 8:36).

PRAYER

Messiah Jesus, You came "to bind up the brokenhearted, to proclaim freedom for the captives and release from darkness the prisoners" (Isa. 61:1). In Your sovereignty, grab the hearts of those who do not yet know You, and open their eyes to Your truth. Help me as well to have a heart for the captives—those who walk in spiritual darkness. Help the Jewish people, Israel, and those around the world who do not yet know You to seek You with all their hearts. May they be found by You. In Messiah's Name, Amen.

JEWISH PEOPLE AND PERSECUTION

I WILL NO LONGER DRIVE OUT BEFORE THEM ANY OF THE NATIONS JOSHUA LEFT WHEN HE DIED. I WILL USE THEM TO TEST ISRAEL AND SEE WHETHER THEY WILL KEEP THE WAY OF THE LORD AND WALK IN IT AS THEIR FOREFATHERS DID.

JUDGES 2:21-22

My people have faced persecution for thousands of years, yet there are many examples of God's protection of them. One such story is that of Hanukkah, the celebration of His protection during the Syrian occupation of Jerusalem in 165 BC.

Antiochus was a king demanding to be worshipped, but the Jewish people would not bow to him. Against all odds, a small band of Jewish zealots, known as the Maccabees, defeated the great Syrian army. Then they rededicated God's temple to the worship of the one true God of Abraham, Isaac, and Jacob.

Yet this was not the first time the Jewish people were targeted—nor the last! Over millennia my people have been targeted by nations such as the Canaanites, the Philistines, the Babylonians, the Syrians, the Iranians; and individuals such as Haman, Antiochus, Hadrian, and Hitler, just to name a few. Jewish people have been persecuted, and even targeted for annihilation, over and over again. And it's still happening today.

Often people ask why the Jewish people have faced such persecution. Why have they been scoffed at, blamed for the world's problems, gathered into ghettos, kicked out of countries, dispersed throughout the world, loaded into railroad cars, huddled into gas chambers to be murdered, and ultimately incinerated in ovens? Why the Jews?

The answer lies in God Word, for the Lord chose to reveal Himself to the world through the Jewish people, and has chosen to use the nations surrounding Israel to reveal Himself to the Jewish people. He chose them to be the Old Covenant people through whom His promises would come, and later the New Covenant also was ushered in through them.

My people have been targeted and persecuted because they are a special people, and the Enemy knows that to destroy them is to destroy the promises of God. Their persecution is not a reflection of God, but a reflection of humanity's sinfulness and need for Him. And so for them, and for all of us, God intends that through the persecution and struggles of life we will see Him and turn to His provision of hope and salvation. He is a God who has always used the surrounding nations to bring restoration to Israel. He has done it before, and He will do it again in the future.

PRAYER

God of Promises, thank You that You are faithful. You are a sovereign God who promises to use the nations to get Israel's attention. You will use the circumstances that surround me, those of my own life, to get my attention as well. Please help the Jewish people to understand that You want their attention, and that You love them. The persecution they have endured is not a reflection on You, but on the world. In the midst of the hostility, help them to turn back to You. In Messiah's Name, Amen.

✡

GOD'S FAITHFULNESS SHOWN THROUGH THE JEWISH PEOPLE

I ASK THEN: DID GOD REJECT HIS PEOPLE?
BY NO MEANS!

ROMANS 1 1:1

In Jeremiah God says through the prophet: "He who appoints the sun to shine by day, who decrees the moon and the stars to shine by night, who stirs up the seas so that its waves roar—the LORD Almighty is His name: 'Only if these decrees vanish from my sight,' declares the LORD, 'will the descendants of Israel ever cease to be a nation before me'" (Jer. 31:35-36).

Thus, the Jewish people can never be destroyed. Their enemies can never wipe Israel off of the face of the earth despite repeated attempts. God gave His promise in His Word to always protect His first loved, and the continuing existence of the Jewish people is one of the greatest testimonies to the existence of God Himself, for if He did not exist, neither would the Jewish people. His covenants are still in effect, and though the Jews, as a people, have turned their back on their Messiah, God promises that Israel as a nation—as a people—will never be destroyed.

Though Jews often have been targeted for annihilation at the hands of their many enemies, they have not only survived, but also thrived. Though many have tried to destroy them, and will continue to do so, the Jewish people stand as an example of God's faithfulness to His promises.

Being a special people, and a people who are opposed, often go hand in hand. The Enemy is well aware of God's love for Israel. Satan, the Destroyer, was well aware that to annihilate the Jewish people before the birth of Jesus would be to eradicate the very lineage through whom the Messiah would come, and that to eradicate them now would undermine God's prophetic plan. While many attempts have been made, none have been successful.

God's promises and covenants began with the Jewish people. And in Deuteronomy we read of our promise-keeping God: "The LORD did not set his affection on you and choose you because you were more numerous than other peoples, for you were the fewest of all peoples. But it was because the LORD loved you and kept the oath he swore to your forefathers that he brought you out with a mighty hand and redeemed you from the land of slavery, from the power of Pharaoh king of Egypt" (Deut. 7:7-8).

His covenants are true, and His promises always kept. The Jewish people stand as a testimony of His faithfulness.

PRAYER

God of faithfulness, thank You for protecting the Jewish people and for showing Yourself true through them. I stand in awe of the way You have revealed Yourself through creation and through the promises of the Old Testament. Help me to remember that You are the God of Creation, the God of Israel, and my God as well. I trust in Your faithfulness to me today. In Jesus' Name, Amen.

GOD'S SALVATION SHOWN THROUGH THE JEWISH PEOPLE

FROM JUDAH WILL COME THE CORNERSTONE,
FROM HIM THE TENT PEG,
FROM HIM THE BATTLE BOW, FROM HIM EVERY RULER.

ZECHARIAH 10:4

Salvation is from the Jews. Jesus made this very clear when he said to the woman at the well, "You Samaritans worship what you do not know; we worship what we do know, for salvation is from the Jews" (John 4:22). It was God's design and purpose to send salvation to us through a Jewish Messiah, and what Jesus was pointing out to the Samaritan woman was that He fit the bill.

Two thousand years ago—a Jewish mother, a Jewish father, and a Jewish baby in a manger—the Messiah was born. Because God protected the lineage of the Messiah from countless attempts of cutting it off, the Messiah was born in Bethlehem, and thus salvation was given to us in the form of a Jewish baby. Thank God for His promises. Thank God for His faithfulness. Thank God that we can see His faithfulness and promises in the existence of His first chosen people—the Jews.

God's promise to use the Jewish people to bring His salvation immediately brought opposition from the Enemy. His promise to use the Jews as an example of His existence and to show Himself faithful through them raised the intensity of Satan's anger. So the spiritual battle ensued, and my people have been at its center for millennia.

The Jewish people have been persecuted because they are a special people—a called out people. Though my people have been disobedient to God, His love for them has never wavered. They have been persecuted because the Enemy knows that though he can never destroy them completely, he will continue to try, in order to make God out to be the liar. Also, the Jewish people have been persecuted because Satan knows that Jesus is going to return to Jerusalem, the city of the Jews, to establish His kingdom. Jesus, He who was born in a lowly manger, and He who died on a cruel cross, will return as King.

PRAYER

Abba, Father, thank You that You have protected the Jewish people from destruction. Thank You that despite the many attempts of the Enemy to destroy Your special people, they survive and exist as an example of Your love and faithfulness. We love You, and we love them. We pray that the Jews would cease to be angry over what has happened to them, and would turn instead to You, looking to You as their only hope of help and deliverance. In Messiah's Name, Amen.

וְאָהַבְתָּ אֵת
Love

יְהוָה אֱלֹהֶיךָ
your God · the LORD

בְּכָל־לְבָבְךָ
your heart · with all

וּבְכָל־נַפְשְׁךָ
your soul · and with all

וּבְכָל־מְאֹדֶךָ
your strength · and with all

"HEAR, O ISRAEL"

SHEMA YISRAEL, ADONAI ELOHEINU, ADONAI ECHAD.

DEUTERONOMY 6:4, HEBREW

HEAR, O ISRAEL: THE LORD OUR GOD,
THE LORD IS ONE.

DEUTERONOMY 6:4

The Shema, Hebrew for *hear*, is the watchword of the Jewish people—the Scripture every Jewish person learns as a child. It is recited daily in the synagogue and is comprised of three biblical passages: Deuteronomy 6:4-9 and 11:13-21, as well as Numbers 15:37-41. It is recited as a prayer morning and evening: "When you lie down and when you get up" (Deut. 6:7).

The Shema, in its essence, presents Judaism's basic tenets—the oneness of God, the love of God and obedience to His commandments, the study of His Word, the principle of divine reward and punishment, and the righteousness that comes from serving Him. Upon reciting the Shema, religious Jewish people cover their eyes with their hands, or cover their heads with their prayer shawls (or tallis), in order to block out the surrounding world and focus on the oneness of the God of Israel. To recite the Shema is to remember God, and is at the heart of the religious Jew.

The Shema, however, is not only a call of the Jewish people to God, but it is also a call from God to the Jewish people. Jesus taught this when asked by the Pharisees, "Teacher, which is the greatest commandment in the Law?" (Matt. 22:36). The Messiah then recited the Shema: "Love the Lord your God with all your heart and with all your soul and with all your mind" (v. 37), but added, "Love your neighbor as yourself" (v. 39). Jesus was warning the Pharisees to put God first—admonishing the Jewish leaders of His day to put the love of God and others before all things. And He was refocusing the rabbis on this truth, which He called the "greatest commandment" (v. 38). Messiah has called my people, and everyone, to a higher standard—one that can only be satisfied in Him.

PRAYER

As Jewish people pray the Shema daily, O Lord, they cover their eyes, attempting to focus on You. Yet it's so easy to miss You in the midst of our religion. It's so easy to focus on the law, but forget its purpose; to get caught up in doing, and miss our surroundings. I so easily lose my focus as well Lord. My mind wanders and many times I forget You are even near. Help me to be different today. Help me to see You more clearly and to love others more deeply. In Messiah's Name, Amen.

PROPHECY INTERPRETED

[GOD] SAID, "GO AND TELL THIS PEOPLE:
'BE EVER HEARING, BUT NEVER UNDERSTANDING; BE
EVER SEEING, BUT NEVER PERCEIVING. MAKE
THE HEART OF THIS PEOPLE CALLOUSED; MAKE
THEIR EYES DULL AND CLOSE THEIR EYES. OTHERWISE
THEY MIGHT SEE WITH THEIR EYES, AND HEAR
WITH THEIR EARS, UNDERSTAND WITH THEIR
HEARTS, AND TURN AND BE HEALED.'"

ISAIAH 6:9-10

Often Christians don't understand why most Jewish people don't believe in Jesus, while, at the same time, many Jewish people wonder why Christians do believe in Him. One of the most important missions of the Messiah, at least from a religious Jewish perspective, was to bring peace to the world. Since Jesus did not bring the earthly peace they expected, the rabbis and leaders of His day rejected Him. And till this day, and for this reason, the Jewish community believes Jesus cannot be the answer.

When a religious Jew reads a messianic prophecy, they may agree with Christians that it is speaking of the Messiah. However, they believe the Messiah mentioned cannot be Jesus. Others may say the same passage is not referring to the Messiah at all—that it is speaking of the nation of Israel (such as how many interpret Isaiah 53), or of a king or ruler of Israel (such as how they interpret Isaiah 7:14 and Micah 5:2). In essence, many approach the prophecies of the Jewish Scriptures as though there are several possible interpretations—something like a multiple-choice test. Yet Jesus would not be on their list of possible answers at all. In their thinking, He simply does not fit, and has been written out of their possibilities. Thus, their interpretation is like trying to put a square peg in a round hole—even if they do have to sand down the edges a bit.

The Jewish rabbis have a personal stake in this, for if Jesus is the Messiah, then they have been incorrect for 2000 years. And it is not easy to admit that one is wrong, especially on such an important issue. God has caused a temporary blindness to come upon Israel, yet by God's grace, and through the power of His Holy Spirit, the eyes of some Jews have been opened. In Jesus' day, many "would not confess their faith … for they loved praise from men more than praise from God" (John 12:42-43). However, many are coming to faith in Him today, for as the Lord said through Jeremiah, "You will seek me and find me when you seek me with all your heart" (Jer. 29:13).

PRAYER

Father, open the eyes of the Jewish people to see You in the prophecies. You, and only You, can open them. Help them to "see with their eyes, hear with their ears, understand with their hearts, and turn and be healed." Please do it, Lord. In Messiah's Name, Amen.

THE SEED OF THE WOMAN

AND I WILL PUT ENMITY
BETWEEN YOU AND THE WOMAN,
AND BETWEEN YOUR SEED AND HER SEED.
GENESIS 3:15, NKJV

This is the first prophecy of the Messiah in the Scriptures. God did not waste any time giving us His description of the Savior here in Genesis 3. This prophecy, known as the Protoevangelium (or the First Gospel), comes from this ancient verse that the Lord proclaimed when He found Adam and Eve guilty of sin. God spoke the words to Satan, who had enticed "the woman" (Eve) into disobeying the Lord's command against eating fruit from "the tree of the knowledge of good and evil" (Gen. 2:9). God goes on to say, "He will crush your head, and you will strike his heel" (Gen. 3:15), meaning that someday Satan will be crushed—that is, utterly defeated by the seed of "the woman."

The coming conqueror had to be a man. But why is He referred to as the seed of a woman, when it is so common for a child to be regarded as the seed of his father and forefathers? This striking and seemingly unnatural expression, "her Seed," suggests that it is a uniquely fitting name for the victor over Satan. Unlike other men, the Messiah would be the seed of a woman—not the seed of a man. A virgin would conceive Him without losing her virginity.

Centuries later, God, through the prophet Isaiah proclaimed, "The

Lord himself will give you a sign: The virgin will be with child and will give birth to a son, and will call him Immanuel" (Isa. 7:14). God was faithful to bring us the Messiah through the seed of a woman—an unnatural occurrence from a human perspective, but a promise from God that He fulfilled in His Son Jesus!

PRAYER

Dear Lord, I thank You that Your promises are true, and that You are a "faithful God, keeping [Your] covenant of love to a thousand generations" (Deut. 7:9). I thank You for Your promises to Israel, especially that Messiah was born of the seed of a woman. You are a great God! I pray that the eyes of Israel and the Jewish people will be opened to the truth of Your Son, Yeshua, born of a virgin. I love and praise You! Amen.

THE CRUCIFIXION PSALM

MY GOD, MY GOD WHY HAVE YOU FORSAKEN ME?
PSALM 22:1

When Jesus was on the cross He quoted Scripture, and not just some random Scripture. As He hung from the cross, with His hands and feet nailed to it, a crown of thorns on His head, and His joints stretched from their sockets, these words came from His lips: "My God, my god, why have you forsaken me?" In great agony, He asked His Father why He felt so distant—so far away. In His humanity, the Messiah cried out to God the Father as He took our sins upon Himself. There were then—and still are today—some Jewish leaders who questioned that cry of Jesus from the cross. Perhaps worse, the Roman soldiers standing nearby mocked and laughed.

Yet if He truly was the Messiah, why did He cry out in that way? Previously Jesus had said, "I have the authority to lay [My life] down and authority to take it up again" (John 10:18), so if He indeed was that powerful, why didn't He just come down from the cross? This powerful King—mocked and ridiculed—chose to remain on the cross. Certainly, He could have come down from there, and with one wave of His hand could have slain them all. But He stayed there, surely dying with great sadness in His eyes, even asking His Father to forgive them (see Luke 23:34).

Through this brief cry from the cross, Jesus, in the most magnificent of ways, was highlighting the remainder of Psalm 22. It was a cry for those who could see—to indeed see—for He was pointing to Himself. "I am poured out like water, and all of my bones are out of joint. My heart has turned to wax; it has melted away within me. My strength is dried up like a potsherd, and my tongue sticks to the roof of my mouth; you lay me in the dust of death. Dogs have surrounded me; a band of evil men has encircled me, they have pierced my hands and my feet. I can count all my bones; people stare and gloat over me" (Ps. 22:14-17).

As Jesus was dying, He knew exactly what to say. This messianic Psalm of David was His words and thoughts of His death, written long before it ever happened—long before crucifixion became a method of capital punishment. And, crucifixion was never a form of Jewish capital punishment. Yet He died on a cross just as the Psalmist predicted.

PRAYER

Messiah, thank You that You hung on a tree for me. Thank You, Father, that through Your Word and infinite wisdom You gave us a picture of Messiah's death, long before it ever happened. You are an amazing God! Help me to remember what Your Son did for me that day. And thank You, Jesus, that You cried out to show me who You are. In Your Name, Amen.

"You, Bethlehem…"

BUT YOU, BETHLEHEM EPHRATHAH, THOUGH
YOU ARE SMALL AMONG THE CLANS OF JUDAH,
OUT OF YOU WILL COME FOR ME ONE WHO WILL
BE RULER OVER ISRAEL, WHOSE ORIGINS ARE FROM
OLD, FROM ANCIENT TIMES.

MICAH 5:2

Jesus was not born in just any town in Israel, but was born in Bethlehem, just as foretold. That's where the Messiah had to be born. Yet His mother and father weren't planning on having Him there, for they were from Nazareth. Certainly they expected their son would be born in the city where they lived, but they unexpectedly got called out of town for a census. Joseph, "because he belonged to the house and line of David" (Luke 2:4), had to return to his hometown to register with the Roman authorities. And so they went. Obviously, God had another plan.

While in Bethlehem, the Messiah was born. The inns were full, so He was born in a place reserved for the animals, probably one of the many caves in the area used by shepherds to this day, or possibly in an area attached to a house or inn, where livestock would have been kept. The Messiah was born exactly where God through the prophet Micah said He would be born.

Nearly 1000 years before the birth of the Messiah, God had made a promise to David, Israel's king who also had been born in Bethlehem. Through the prophet Nathan he said, "Your house and your kingdom will endure forever before me; your throne will be established forever" (2 Sam. 7:16). David's throne "established forever"—Joseph from "the house … of David"—the Messiah born in Bethlehem—His throne "established forever"!

In Hebrew, Bethlehem means "house of bread," so it is no coincidence that Jesus, the Son of David, said, "The bread of God is he who comes down from heaven and gives life to the world. … I am the bread of life" (John 6:33, 35). "The Bread of Life"—born in Bethlehem, the house of bread.

PRAYER

Lord of the Universe, thank You for Your prophecies that show us who our Messiah is. You foretold that David's throne would last forever—throughout eternity. David was a mere mortal man, and yet his throne was promised to last forever. Thank You that He was born at just the right time in just the right place—David's throne established through the Son of David. Eternal and forever. My "bread of life," born in the house of bread. I love You. In Your Name, Amen.

CREATOR OF THE FRUIT OF THE VINE

BLESSED ARE YOU, OH LORD OUR GOD, KING OF THE
UNIVERSE, CREATOR OF THE FRUIT OF THE VINE.
(ANCIENT JEWISH BLESSING OVER THE WINE)

It is no coincidence that Jesus' first miracle was at a wedding in Cana.
And, of course, it was a Jewish wedding. He chose that place and
that time to begin His earthly ministry in full power, and He chose
the creation of wine as His first display of that miraculous power.

Jesus' mother and brothers were there as well, and as the wedding
reception went on, they ran out of wine. Being the Jewish wedding that
it was, more wine was necessary to continue the celebration. In biblical,
and in Jewish thought, a full cup represents complete joy! The psalmist
David wrote, "My cup overflows" (Ps. 23:5), indicating the overflow
of abundant blessing. But, now the wine was gone, and Jesus' mother
came to Him to let Him know. At first Jesus was hesitant, saying to His
mother that He really didn't want to be involved: "My time has not yet
come" (John 2:4).

But then Jesus acted, instructing the servants to fill six stone water
jars with water. He surely would have said a blessing. We don't know
what the blessing was, but turning water into wine was certainly the
opportune time to say one. Perhaps He said the ancient Jewish blessing,

"Baruk atah Adonai, Elohaynu melek haolam, boray peri hagaafen"—Blessed are You, oh Lord our God, King of the universe, Creator of the fruit of the vine." This is the ancient blessing over the wine, and is the recognition that only God can create the fruit of the vine. He is the only One powerful enough to change the elements. And Jesus did it! He changed water into wine, and in so doing, proclaimed Himself the divine Messiah.

"This, the first of his miraculous signs, Jesus performed at Cana in Galilee. He thus revealed his glory, and his disciples put their faith in him" (John 2:11). Only a Jewish mom could get her son to start His ministry like that!

PRAYER

Creator of the universe, I thank You that You showed Yourself to us in Messiah Jesus. I am blessed today because of You. I truly can say that "my cup overflows" with Your blessings, not because of my circumstances, but because of who You are in my life. Help me to see Your miracles in a special way today. You can change the elements, and You can change me. I love You. In Jesus' Name, Amen.

ISAIAH 53

WHO HAS BELIEVED OUR MESSAGE AND TO WHOM HAS THE ARM OF THE LORD BEEN REVEALED?

ISAIAH 53:1

My testimony is like many other Jewish people. I was raised in a religious Jewish home, and was told that one cannot be Jewish and believe in Jesus. I was told that Jesus is the "Christian God." I had no understanding of the messianic prophecies in the Old Testament, because we did not study the Bible. When I went to synagogue, five days a week, every week from the ages of six to fifteen, I studied the religion of Judaism. I learned about the Jewish festivals, I heard the Torah chanted in Hebrew on Saturday mornings, and I studied the prayer book and trained for my upcoming Bar Mitzvah when I would turn twelve.

I was taught about the Messiah, but that the Jewish people are still waiting for Him to come. He will not be God, they said, but He will be a righteous man who will come to bring peace to the world. I was told that when Messiah comes that "The wolf will live with the lamb, the leopard will lie down with the goat, the calf and the lion and the yearling together; and a little child will lead them." (Isa. 11:6) that "they will beat their swords into plowshares … nor will they train for war anymore" (Isa. 2:4), and that the Messiah will rebuild the temple, gather the Jewish people back to the land of Israel, and ultimately establish His messianic kingdom. That's what I learned, and it is what Jewish people are taught today. I was told all these things were in the Bible, but was never told where.

Yet when I went to college I began to search for God for myself. I believed in Him, but, in my heart, I knew I did not know who He was. For me, God was an untouchable, unreachable entity in the cosmos. He was distant. But somehow, I knew that He also was knowable. And I wanted to know Him. So I began my search. I found a Bible and began to read. God placed some Christians across the hall from me in my dorm, and they pointed me in the direction of the messianic prophecies in the Old Testament. And as I read Isaiah 53, it was then that God began to open my eyes.

Most often, it is this passage—Isaiah 53—that touches the heart of a Jewish person searching for God. Through it, a passage written 700 years before Jesus, God gives us a clear description of what the Messiah would do when He came to earth.

PRAYER

God of Israel, help Jewish people to see You in Isaiah 53. Please take them to this passage and open their eyes. Thank You that You so clearly give us a picture—a clear description of Jesus—in this chapter. Thank You that Your Word is true and that the Jewish prophets of old spoke of Messiah to come. In His Name, Amen.

MESSIAH WILL SUFFER

HE WAS DESPISED AND REJECTED BY MEN, A MAN OF
SORROWS, AND FAMILIAR WITH SUFFERING.
LIKE ONE FROM WHOM MEN HIDE THEIR FACES HE WAS
DESPISED, AND WE ESTEEMED HIM NOT.

ISAIAH 53:3

The concept of a suffering messiah is not foreign to Jewish thought. The orthodox rabbis teach of a messiah, the son of David (Messiah ben David), and of another messiah, the son of Joseph (Messiah ben Joseph). Messiah ben David is the conquering messiah, the one to bring peace to the world and usher in the messianic kingdom. Messiah ben Joseph is the suffering messiah. According to the rabbis, Messiah ben Joseph will suffer, and will die prior to the reign of Messiah ben David, who will rule over the messianic kingdom. They teach two messiahs, but each with a different purpose.

I vaguely understood the concepts of the suffering Messiah and the kingly Messiah when I was growing up, but to most Jewish people who are waiting for the Messiah today, they are waiting for Messiah ben David, the conquering messiah to come and bring peace to the world. Two thousand years ago my Jewish people were waiting for a king as well. They were hoping for the conquering messiah to save them from Roman oppression. They were waiting for the messianic kingdom of peace to be established. They were waiting for a savior.

Jesus did not come to bring the peace for which they were looking. He came to bear the sins of my people, as well as people around the world. He came as the rejected Messiah, and that rejection was for the purpose of bringing peace between man and God. Though our sins separate us from God, Jesus endured pain on our behalf as the Messiah. He came to suffer and die, one day He will return to establish His kingdom on earth, and to bring everlasting peace.

PRAYER

Jesus, we look for peace in our circumstances, and we want the world around us to be without conflict. But Your Word tells us, "In this world you will have trouble" (John 16:33). Help me to remember that true peace is being in Your presence, and is not simply the absence of conflict. Help me to rest in Your peace today, and to remember that You came to suffer first to bring me into relationship with Your Father in order to have Your spiritual peace. Thank You for being my Messiah. In Your Name, Amen.

MESSIAH WILL CARRY OUR SINS

BUT HE WAS PIERCED FOR OUR TRANSGRESSIONS,
HE WAS CRUSHED FOR OUR INIQUITIES;
THE PUNISHMENT THAT BROUGHT US PEACE WAS
UPON HIM, AND BY HIS WOUNDS WE ARE HEALED.

ISAIAH 53:5

Messiah's suffering was for a purpose. According to Scripture His suffering was for "our transgressions" and "our iniquities." The idea that the Messiah would carry our sins is foreign to Jewish people today, just as it was for the Jewish community of Jesus' day. It is much easier to look for someone to save us from external trouble, when the real trouble is within us. The first issue that had to be addressed by the Messiah was the issue of sin, arrogance, pride, self-sufficiency, and a lack of faith in God. No people, including my people, would be able to live up to His holy standards. Separation from God due to our fallen condition was much worse than physical bondage at the hands of the Roman kingdom.

Jesus was born into a Jewish society that was rattled by Roman occupation and oppression. How easy it was for the Jewish community to be blind to their need for spiritual redemption! As the Romans ruled over them and occupied their land they looked for someone to free them from their external dilemma. Their hope was that the Messiah would overcome their visible circumstances and usher in the earthly kingdom of peace.

Jesus told the Jewish rulers of His day, "My kingdom is not of this world" (John 18:36). He did not come to save my people from Roman oppression 2000 years ago. He came to save them from their own sin, and to extend that salvation to Gentiles as well. Jesus said He did not come to give peace "as the world gives" (John 14:27), but to bring true shalom—peace between man and God.

Through Jesus' suffering and death, peace comes to "everyone who believes: first for the Jew, then for the Gentile" (Rom. 1:16). By the wounds of Jesus, the Jewish Messiah, true peace can be a reality.

PRAYER

Thank You, Jesus, for dying for me. Please help the Jewish people see who You are, and that You came to bear their sins and the sins of others around the world. I love You for what You endured for me. Open the eyes of those around me who do not yet know You. In Your Name, Amen.

MESSIAH WILL RISE FROM THE DEAD

AFTER THE SUFFERING OF HIS SOUL, HE WILL SEE
THE LIGHT [OF LIFE] AND BE SATISFIED; BY HIS
KNOWLEDGE MY RIGHTEOUS SERVANT WILL JUSTIFY
MANY, AND HE WILL BEAR THEIR INIQUITIES.

ISAIAH 53:11

It is truly amazing that the Scriptures so clearly speak of the resurrection of the Messiah. After His death for our sins, the Bible says that He will "see the light [of life] and be satisfied." Evidence of the Messiah's power over sin would be His power over death. We are told that the suffering Messiah would suffer, that after His suffering He would die, be buried in a rich man's tomb, and then rise from the dead.

Belief in the concept of resurrection is fundamental to Orthodox Judaism. The great twelfth century Jewish commentator Maimonides, who wrote the "13 Principles of Faith," included believing in the resurrection as the thirteenth principle. He concluded that both the one who denies the concept of the resurrection of the dead, or the one who denies the coming of the Messiah, are among those who have forfeited their share in Olam Ha-ba—the hereafter, or "the world to come" (Mishneh Torah Hilkhot Teshuvah 3:6). The rabbis teach that one day there will be a resurrection of all people who know God into His eternal kingdom. However, the rabbis do not teach that the Messiah will be raised from the dead. Resurrection of the righteous is seen as an event that will happen at the end of time, part of the culmination of world history.

Yet Jesus fulfilled the prophecy of Messiah's resurrection in Isaiah 53. The apostle Paul wrote to the church in Corinth, "Christ [the Messiah] has indeed been raised from the dead, the firstfruits of those who have fallen asleep" (1 Cor. 15:20). Though the Jewish leaders of Jesus' day rejected His resurrection, it was prophesied by the prophet Isaiah, and is the foundation of faith in Jesus. Belief in the resurrection of the dead is fundamental to Judaism and belief in the resurrection of Jesus is fundamental to Christianity. Without the fulfilled prophecy of resurrection, faith in Jesus as Messiah is meaningless. His resurrection proves the validity of His truth.

PRAYER

You rose from the dead, Messiah Jesus. Because You rose, You give me new life. Your resurrection showed Your power over death. And it shows the truth and faithfulness of the Father. Because You triumphed over the grave, I can know You and also know the power of Your resurrection. I thank You that You rose for me. Please help me to help others recognize that same power. Amen!

FESTIVALS OF ISRAEL

THE LORD SAID TO MOSES, "SPEAK TO THE ISRAELITES AND SAY TO THEM: 'THESE ARE MY APPOINTED FEASTS, THE APPOINTED FEASTS OF THE LORD, WHICH YOU ARE TO PROCLAIM AS SACRED ASSEMBLIES.'"

LEVITICUS 23:1-2

God gave the Jewish festivals to His chosen people primarily to set them apart. Like all the commandments given to the Israelites in the Old Testament, God instituted the festivals so that when the Jewish people celebrated those holidays, they would look different from the pagans who worshiped other Gods. And, when the Israelites celebrated the God of Israel, He wanted the surrounding nations to see Him through those Jewish festivals. The festivals were also a call to worship and obedience, some requiring a sacrifice, but all of them requiring obedience to God's commands.

There are eight festivals mentioned in Leviticus 23. One of them is a weekly festival, the Sabbath, and it required rest from work on the seventh day of each week, to remember that God rested and enjoyed His own creation. In the same way, we are commanded to rest and enjoy God. There also are seven yearly festivals, four in the spring and three in the fall. They are Passover, Unleavened Bread, Firstfruits, Weeks (Pentecost), the Festival of Trumpets, the Day of Atonement, and the Feast of Tabernacles.

Jesus fulfilled the spring holidays on the very day of the festival when He was here on earth. His blood was shed on Passover; His body was crucified, or broken, on the Feast of Unleavened Bread; He was raised from the dead on Firstfruits; and His Spirit was poured out on Pentecost. But upon His return, He will fulfill the fall festivals, for the Festival of Trumpets looks forward to His return, the Day of Atonement to His judgment, and the Feast of Tabernacles to the establishment of His kingdom. The entire life and ministry of Jesus, the Messiah, can be seen from beginning to end in the precise order of the Jewish festivals in Leviticus 23.

PRAYER

God of the Jewish festivals, thank You for the clarity of Your Word. You so clearly show us who You are through the festivals. Jesus, You are not hidden, but revealed, through the holidays that were so important to You. I love You for showing Yourself to me in this way. In Messiah's Name, Amen.

PASSOVER FREEDOM

THE LORD'S PASSOVER BEGINS AT TWILIGHT ON THE FOURTEENTH DAY OF THE FIRST MONTH.
LEVITICUS 23:5

If there is one holiday celebrated by all Jewish people it is Passover. Like our American Thanksgiving, Passover is the holiday that brings the Jewish family together. I remember celebrating Passover with my family, when thirty of us would gather at my aunt and uncle's house. My grandparents, aunts, uncles, and cousins from around the country would come to celebrate. When the table was set, we would read from the ancient Hagaddah, the telling of the story of the Exodus, and enjoy a huge meal together.

Just as most Americans do not see God in Thanksgiving, most Jewish people do not see the God of Israel in the Passover. And in the same way that Christmas has become a secular holiday for those who are simply cultural "Christians," Passover has become a secular holiday for most Jewish people, who are secular, non-religious Jews. It is not unusual for Jewish family members to sit at the Passover table and celebrate the holiday, not believing in the God of the Bible or the story of the Exodus itself. In a similar way, many around the world celebrate the birth of Jesus without truly believing in the God of the Bible, or in the birth of His Son. Churches are filled to overflowing on Easter with many denying the truth of the resurrection.

However, for the religious Jewish person, Passover is a night to remember the "mighty hand" of God who redeemed my people from slavery and bondage to Egyptian oppression. Yes, "The LORD brought us out of Egypt with a mighty hand and an outstretched arm" (Deut. 26:8). It is about freedom and redemption, for the Passover message of redemption is found in the way He did redeem His people—through the blood of the Lamb.

Just as Americans should be thankful at Thanksgiving for being free from British rule, all believers in Jesus—whether Jewish or Gentile—should be thankful at Passover, and always, not simply for freedom from bondage to Egyptian rule, but for the spiritual freedom we have in the Passover Lamb.

PRAYER

God of freedom, I thank You for the hope I have through my Messiah, the Passover Lamb. I thank You for the story of freedom and redemption that can only be mine through Your act of strength. You battled for me and personally freed me from oppression. Thank You for Your "mighty hand and ... outstretched arm." In Your Mighty Name, Amen.

THE PASSOVER LAMB

THE BLOOD WILL BE A SIGN FOR YOU ON
THE HOUSES WHERE YOU ARE;
AND WHEN I SEE THE BLOOD, I WILL PASS OVER YOU.
EXODUS 12:13

One of the most significant holidays on the Jewish calendar is Passover—the festival commemorating God's redemption of the Israelites from slavery and bondage to Pharaoh in Egypt. During the tenth plague against the Egyptians, God commanded the Israelites to place the blood of a perfect lamb on the doorposts of their homes. Because of that blood, death passed over them. Thus, Passover demonstrates God's love for the Jewish people and His promise to fulfill His covenant with them.

Jesus chose the Passover as His last meal, yet little did the disciples realize its significance. Jesus had entered Jerusalem on a colt. Messianic expectations were high for some, while political ambitions were on the minds of others. Roman authorities were concerned about keeping control over their territory, while Jewish leaders were focused on maintaining their control over Judaism. And Jesus was caught in the middle.

He and His disciples went through an order of service called a Seder, meaning *order*. All of the festival elements were on Jesus' table, in keeping with God's instructions to Moses. Throughout all generations

Israel was to commemorate their redemption from slavery in Egypt, having on their tables the Passover lamb, unleavened bread, bitter herbs, and the fruit of the vine. Thus, Jesus too focused His disciples on the story of redemption, just as Jewish people do today during the Passover celebration.

Yet that Passover was different. After the meal, during the third cup—the Cup of Redemption—Jesus did something He had never done before. He lifted the cup, along with some unleavened bread; looked at His disciples; and said, in essence, "This is all about Me" (see Luke 22:20). The Jewish Messiah, with his Jewish disciples, in a Jewish land, was celebrating a Jewish festival—the Passover—and teaching His disciples His ultimate purpose in coming to earth.

PRAYER

Thank you, Jesus, that You are my Passover Lamb. Your blood was shed, and Your body broken, for me. You came to suffer and die for me, and for people of all the nations of the world, so that spiritual death would "pass over" all who believe. I love You for what You did for me on the cross. In Your Name, Amen.

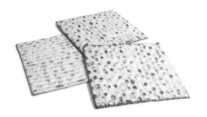

UNLEAVENED BREAD

ON THE FIFTEENTH DAY OF THAT MONTH THE LORD'S
FEAST OF UNLEAVENED BREAD BEGINS;
FOR SEVEN DAYS YOU MUST EAT BREAD MADE
WITHOUT YEAST.

LEVITICUS 23:6

During the six weeks before the Festival of Passover, Jewish homes undergo a complete "spring cleaning." Everything containing leaven, or yeast, is removed from the home. In homes of the most religious Jews, even the books are shaken out, just in case a crumb of bread might have fallen into it while reading. In the less religious homes, the leaven is put into bags and put in the basement to be taken out later.

Just before Passover a few crumbs are left in a corner of the home. The head of the household, usually the father, takes a wooden spoon, a candle, and a feather and then searches for the crumbs. The ceremony is called Bedikat Chametz, meaning "the searching for the leaven." Once the crumbs are found, they are swept into the wooden spoon with the feather, wrapped in a cloth, and burned. The home is now free from leaven and ready for the Feast of Unleavened Bread.

In the Bible leaven is a symbol of sin because it "puffs up" everything coming into contact with it. This is why Paul wrote, "A little yeast works through the whole batch of dough" (1 Cor. 5:6). But unleavened bread is made without yeast, and it symbolizes the bread the Israelites ate when they fled in haste from Egypt. Unleavened bread, and the Feast of Unleavened Bread, represents freedom, redemption, purity, and perfection.

In Matthew 26:17-19, we read, "On the first day of the Feast of Unleavened Bread, the disciples came to Jesus and asked, 'Where do you want us to make preparations for you to eat the Passover?' He replied, 'Go into the city to a certain man and tell him, "The Teacher says: My appointed time is near. I am going to celebrate the Passover with my disciples at your house."'" So the disciples did as Jesus had directed them and prepared the Passover."

Jesus sent His disciples to search for the leaven. We don't know exactly how they prepared the home, but in all likelihood they cleaned it and removed the leaven, preparing it for the Unleavened One Himself. Jesus died on the Feast of Unleavened Bread. His perfect body was broken. The perfect Passover Lamb died—for you and for me.

PRAYER

My Passover Lamb, I thank You that Your sinless body was broken for me. The feast of Unleavened Bread is fully symbolized, in Your broken body—stripped, pierced, and afflicted. I am grateful for Your death on a cross. Messiah, may the Jewish people come to know what You did for them and for me. In Your Name, Amen.

FIRSTFRUITS

THE LORD SAID TO MOSES, "SPEAK TO THE ISRAELITES
AND SAY TO THEM: 'WHEN YOU ENTER THE LAND I
AM GOING TO GIVE YOU AND YOU REAP ITS HARVEST,
BRING TO THE PRIEST A SHEAF OF THE FIRST GRAIN
YOU HARVEST.'"

LEVITICUS 23:9-10

Three days after the Festival of Passover (a one night feast) and the beginning of the Feast of Unleavened Bread (which begins the night of Passover) comes another Jewish festival called the Festival of Firstfruits, or S'firat ha'Omer in Hebrew, which means "the counting of the sheaf." It is the early harvest festival on the Jewish calendar. In fact, most of the Hebrew festivals are based on and connected to the agricultural cycle. Early in the spring, the late winter and early spring crops were gathered and brought to the Lord. Typically, these were the firstfruits from the barley harvest of the year. It was an exciting time to thank God for His early provision. Out of the death of winter had come new life and sustenance, and it was a time to rejoice.

It is no coincidence that Jesus was raised from the dead on the very day of the Festival of Firstfruits. Just as his blood was shed as our Passover Lamb on Passover and His sinless body was broken at the beginning of the Feast of Unleavened Bread, His body was raised from the dead on Firstfruits. Paul, in his first letter to the church in Corinth, proclaimed, "But Christ has indeed been raised from the dead, the firstfruits of those who have fallen asleep. For since death came through a man, the resurrection of the dead comes also through a man. For as in Adam all die, so in Christ all will be made alive" (1 Cor. 15:20-22).

Jesus said, "I am the resurrection and the life. He who believes in me will live, even though he dies" (John 11:25). Out of the death of the Messiah—from His crucifixion and agony, His broken Body and poured out blood—comes new life and resurrection for all who believe. Isn't it just like God to raise the Messiah from the dead on the Jewish Festival of Firstfruits?

PRAYER

Jesus, thank You that You defeated death on the Festival of Firstfruits. Out of the agony of Your death, I can know new life. Because You were raised from the dead I can know the joy of spring. Please help me not only t ao rejoice in my new life, but also to take that new life to others who need to hear. Fill me with the power of Your resurrection today! In Messiah's Name, Amen.

FEAST OF WEEKS (PENTECOST)

FROM THE DAY AFTER THE SABBATH, THE DAY YOU
BROUGHT THE SHEAF OF THE WAVE OFFERING,
COUNT OFF SEVEN FULL WEEKS. COUNT OFF FIFTY
DAYS UP TO THE DAY AFTER THE SEVENTH SABBATH,
AND THEN PRESENT AN OFFERING OF NEW GRAIN
TO THE LORD.

LEVITICUS 23:15-16

Fifty days after Passover, God told the Jewish people to have another harvest festival. It comes later in the spring and is known as Shavuot in Hebrew. The English translation of the word is weeks, but most people know the holiday by the Greek word *Pentecost.*

Shavuot is the latter harvest festival each spring. It was one of the three festivals during which the Israelites were commanded to go up to Jerusalem to take their sacrifices to the Lord, with the others being Passover and Yom Kippur, or the Day of Atonement. Firstfruits, the early harvest, consisted primarily of barley, while Shavuot was primarily wheat. Two loaves of bread were to be baked and then waved before the Lord in thanksgiving for a good spring harvest, and in the hope of His continued blessings throughout the summer season.

It was on the very day of this festival that we read in Acts 2 of the outpouring of the Holy Spirit of God on the early Jewish believers in Jesus. They had gathered in Jerusalem in the temple area some time after Jesus had ascended to heaven. On Shavuot, with a rushing of wind and tongues of fire, those believers—waiting, just as they had been instructed by Jesus—were filled with the Holy Spirit of God. It was the power of the Holy Spirit who then enabled them to proclaim the message of Messiah to the other Jewish people gathered in Jerusalem. And thousands of Jewish people were saved that day!

Because of the outpouring of the Holy Spirit on that Jewish festival of Shavuot, the early Jewish believers were given strength, courage, and power to take the message of Jesus to the rest of the world. Some say the wave offering of two loaves represent Jew and Gentile brought together in faith, together grafted into the rich root of the olive tree (see Romans 11:17-24). What a beautiful picture of the body of Messiah! And Shavuot is the Jewish festival that began it all.

PRAYER

God of Power, I thank You for the Jewish festival of Shavuot, or Pentecost. On that day You poured out Your Holy Spirit. You gave power to those early Jewish believers to proclaim Your message of salvation. I am a recipient of Your salvation because of them. Help Jewish people around the world to understand who You are. Open their eyes and fill them with Your Spirit. In Messiah's Name, Amen.

TRUMPETS

THE LORD SAID TO MOSES, "SAY TO THE ISRAELITES:
'ON THE FIRST DAY OF THE SEVENTH MONTH
YOU ARE TO HAVE A DAY OF REST, A SACRED ASSEMBLY
COMMEMORATED WITH TRUMPET BLASTS.
DO NO REGULAR WORK, BUT PRESENT AN OFFERING
MADE TO THE LORD BY FIRE.'"

LEVITICUS 23:23-25

The Bible does not give us a great deal of information on the Festival of Trumpets, or Yom Teruah in Hebrew. We are only told that the Israelites were to hold a sacred assembly and to blow trumpets. The holiday is not connected with an agricultural event, nor is it connected with a historical observance. So, in order for us to understand why trumpets were blown on that day, one must ask, "Why were trumpets typically blown in the Bible?"

In fact, there were several reasons and occasions when trumpets were blown. They were blown in battle, they were blown as a call to assembly, they were blown at the coronation of a king, and they were blown as a call to repentance. The blowing of the shofar, or ram's horn, on the Festival of Trumpets was probably a call to assembly and repentance in preparation for the next holiday on the calendar, The Day of Atonement, or Yom Kippur. Thus, most likely, it was a call to repent, to return to God, to ask for forgiveness, and to pray for His favor.

Most of us who know Jesus, know He is going to return at the sound of a trumpet. We read in the apostle Paul's letter to the church in Thessalonica, "For the Lord himself will come down from heaven, with a loud command, with the voice of the archangel and with the trumpet call of God, and the dead in Christ will rise first" (1 Thess. 4:16). The Messiah is going to call His loved ones to Himself with the sound of the trumpet. On that day we will all assemble, He will bring His judgment to the world, and He will return to establish His kingdom. Jesus Himself will be the fulfillment of the Festival of Trumpets when He returns in His glory.

PRAYER

Messiah of Redemption, thank You that You are going to return at the sound of the great trumpet blast from heaven. You are going to gather Your saints and reign as King. I look forward to the great trumpet call of God. I wait in anticipation for Your return. I ask that You prepare Israel and the Jewish people to receive You. Open their "eyes to see" and their "ears to hear" (Ezek. 12:2) Your call, even as we wait for Your return. In Jesus' Name, Amen.

ROSH HASHANAH A LOOK AT ABRAHAM'S FAITH AND GOD'S FAITHFULNESS

"THE FIRE AND WOOD ARE HERE," ISAAC SAID, "BUT WHERE IS THE LAMB FOR THE BURNT OFFERING?" ABRAHAM ANSWERED, "GOD HIMSELF WILL PROVIDE THE LAMB FOR THE BURNT OFFERING, MY SON."

GENESIS 22:7-8

The shofar (Ram's Horn) is blown in the synagogue heralding the Festival of Trumpets, but it also begins Rosh Hashanah, the Jewish New Year. The haunting sound of the trumpet announces the beginning of the ten Days of Awe, Yomim Nora'im, the ten days of repentance between Rosh Hashanah and the Day of Atonement, Yom Kippur. During this time religious Jewish people are intensely focused on the spiritual and on their need to repent of their sins. They ask forgiveness both from their fellowman and from God.

On Rosh Hashanah, in the synagogue, the rabbi chants from the Torah and recounts the story from Genesis 22—the story of Abraham binding Isaac to the altar. It is known as the Akedah, meaning "The Binding." As Abraham raised his hand to slay his beloved son, an angel stopped him saying, "'Do not lay a hand on the boy.' … There in a thicket he saw a ram caught by its horns," ready to be sacrificed (vv. 12-13).

At the beginning of the rabbinical New Year, Rosh Hashanah, Jewish people remember the faithfulness of God for providing a sacrifice in place of Isaac. The ram's horn is blown as a call to enter the season of repentance as well as to remember God's faithfulness to Abraham.

For those of us who know the Messiah, we look forward to the return of Jesus at the sound of a trumpet. The sound of the shofar, for the Jewish community, is a call to repentance. It is a day to begin preparation for God's judgment. For those of us who have received His forgiveness, the sound of the shofar not only reminds us of God's ultimate sacrifice in His Son, but also reminds us to wait expectantly for His return.

PRAYER

Father, the sound of the shofar, or ram's horn, reminds the Jewish community of their need to repent, and of Your faithfulness to provide a sacrifice. We see in Abraham's faith, and his willingness to sacrifice his son, an example of what You did for us in sacrificing Your son on our behalf. Thank You for giving Him for my salvation. I wait expectantly for the sound of the trumpet from heaven heralding the return of our Messiah and Savior—Jesus!

ABRAHAM PRAISED GOD

ABRAHAM LOOKED UP AND THERE IN A THICKET
HE SAW A RAM CAUGHT BY ITS HORNS.
HE WENT OVER AND TOOK THE RAM AND SACRIFICED
IT AS A BURNT OFFERING INSTEAD OF HIS SON.

GENESIS 22:13

One can only imagine the joy and thankfulness in Abraham's heart as he worshipped God with Isaac—especially after his son had been spared from death! Out of Abraham's belief, faith, and obedience, came praise and blessing.

"The angel of the LORD called to Abraham from heaven a second time and said, 'I swear by myself, declares the LORD, that because you have done this and have not withheld your son, your only son, I will surely bless you and make your descendants as numerous as the stars in the sky and as the sand on the seashore. Your descendants will take possession of the cities of their enemies, and through your offspring all nations on earth will be blessed, because you have obeyed me'" (Gen. 22:15-18).

When we believe God, have faith in God, and obey God, we have every reason to praise God! And as we walk through life, we always should remember Abraham as a godly example. Often God will call us to do things far beyond our personal comfort zone. Sharing our faith is just one of those. Some would rather their right arm be cut off than to have to talk to a friend—let alone a stranger—about Jesus. Especially a Jewish friend! Yet perhaps God is calling you to be like Abraham in an area of your life. Believe Him, obey Him, and praise Him!

Because of Abraham's faith and obedience, God promised him the blessing of being the father of many. Ultimately that promise was fulfilled in the coming of Messiah through Abraham's own lineage. The Jewish people are a part of that promise, for Jesus came to us through Jewish parents. And those of us who know Him are counted as being a part of the blessing of faith. What a great honor to be grafted in!

PRAYER

Lord, You called Abraham to do something not only difficult, but also impossible from my perspective. And yet Abraham believed, obeyed, and then You provided. I thank You for Your provision and for Your faithfulness to me. Thank You that when I obey, You provide. Help me believe and obey today. In Messiah Jesus' Name. Amen

✡

DAY OF ATONEMENT

THE LORD SAID TO MOSES, "THE TENTH DAY OF THIS
SEVENTH MONTH IS THE DAY OF ATONEMENT. HOLD
A SACRED ASSEMBLY AND DENY YOURSELVES, AND
PRESENT AN OFFERING MADE TO THE LORD BY FIRE.
DO NO WORK ON THAT DAY, BECAUSE IT IS A DAY OF
ATONEMENT, WHEN ATONEMENT IS MADE FOR YOU
BEFORE THE LORD YOUR GOD."
LEVITICUS 23: 26-28

Yom Kippur, or the Day of Atonement, is the holiest day of the
Jewish year. On that day, Jewish people around the world ask God
for forgiveness for their sins. It is a day of complete fasting—one
without food or water. It is a day spent in the synagogue, with everyone
standing much of the time. On that day, Jewish people beseech the God
of Abraham, Isaac, and Jacob to write their names in the book of life.
They hope and pray God will forgive them for their sins, be merciful to
them, and pardon them.

The rabbis tell a story, one based on rabbinical Jewish legend, that
when the shofar is blown on the Festival of Trumpets, God opens the
books in heaven to judge the Jewish people. For ten days He judges, and
at the end of the Day of Atonement He closes the books. By that point,
God has written the names of all Jewish people in either the Book of

Life or the Book of Death, determining who will live and who will die, and who will have a good year and who will have strife. Thus, at the end of the Day of Atonement, according to the rabbis, God's judgment has been determined and is pronounced.

This explains why, for the ten days between the Festival of Trumpets and the Day of Atonement, religious Jewish people plead with God to write their names in the Book of Life. When the trumpet is sounded, judgment begins, and when the Day of Atonement ends, judgment is sealed.

Unfortunately, most in the Jewish community today do not understand that the law condemns us all, and that the law can never save us or bring us into a relationship with God. And, as the Scriptures tell us, "Our righteous acts are like filthy rags" (Isa. 64:6). No amount of praying, fasting, or repenting on Yom Kippur will get one's name written in the book of life. Only the Messiah can do that. He came to take our judgment on Himself. He is our kipporah—our covering—before God.

PRAYER

Jesus, thank You that You came that our names may be written in the Book of Life, and that my name is written there! I pray for those who don't yet know You. Open the eyes and the hearts of those who have yet to have their names inscribed in Your Book. I pray for my friends and family. And I ask that You would help the Jewish community to know You, "the author of life" (Acts 3:15), Messiah Jesus. In Your Name, Amen.

THE TRUE SCAPEGOAT

WHEN AARON HAS FINISHED MAKING ATONEMENT
FOR THE MOST HOLY PLACE, THE TENT OF MEETING
AND THE ALTAR, HE SHALL BRING FORWARD THE
LIVE GOAT. HE IS TO LAY BOTH HANDS ON THE HEAD
OF THE LIVE GOAT AND CONFESS OVER IT ALL THE
WICKEDNESS AND REBELLION OF THE ISRAELITES—ALL
THEIR SINS—AND PUT THEM ON THE GOAT'S HEAD. HE
SHALL SEND THE GOAT AWAY INTO THE DESERT IN THE
CARE OF A MAN APPOINTED FOR THE TASK.
LEVITICUS 16:20-21

The Talmud (ancient rabbinical commentary on the Scriptures) discusses numerous remarkable phenomena that occurred in the temple during the Yom Kippur service. One of those mentioned was a strip of scarlet-dyed wool tied to the head of the scapegoat, which would turn white in the presence of the large crowd gathered at the temple on the Day of Atonement. The Jewish people perceived this miraculous transformation as a heavenly sign that their sins were forgiven.

The Talmud relates, however, that forty years before the destruction of the second temple in 70 AD the scarlet colored strip of wool did not turn white. The Talmud states, "The Rabbis taught that forty years prior to the destruction of the temple the lot did not come up in the [high priest's] right hand nor did the tongue of scarlet wool become white…" (Tractate Yoma 39b). Certainly, it can be no coincidence that forty years before the destruction of the temple, Jesus died on the cross for the sins of Israel. He died, taking the place of the scapegoat.

The scapegoat is a picture of God's salvation. Thousands of years before Messiah Jesus came, God, through the scapegoat, gave us a yearly visual of what Jesus came to do. Isaiah said, "We all, like sheep, have gone astray, each of us has turned to his own way; and the LORD has laid on him the iniquity of us all" (Isa. 53:6).

Today, Jewish people who do not know Messiah Jesus hope for forgiveness, hope for pardon, hope God will be merciful to them on the Day of Atonement. They fervently pray, but they do not *know*. The apostle Paul stated, "For I can testify about them that they are zealous for God, but their zeal is not based on knowledge" (Rom. 10:2).

We as believers, who *do know* Jesus as the Messiah, have a responsibility to pray that the Jewish people and Israel will hear that He has come, so that they too might know His eternal life.

PRAYER

Lord Jesus, thank You for being my scapegoat, for taking my sins upon Yourself. I praise You for giving me a picture of who You are through Your Word, and even through traditional Jewish teaching. May those who have yet to know You come to know Your truth. I love You today for dying for me and carrying my sins for me. In Your matchless Name I pray. Amen.

JEWISH ATONEMENT TODAY

"DO YOU SEE ALL THESE THINGS?" HE ASKED.
"I TELL YOU THE TRUTH, NOT ONE STONE HERE
WILL BE LEFT ON ANOTHER; EVERY ONE WILL BE
THROWN DOWN."

MATTHEW 24:2

When the temple was destroyed in 70 AD, as prophesied by Jesus, the sacrificial system ceased. Initially that system was dependent on the existence of the tabernacle, then the temple. Everything connected to the sacrificial system happened within the context of the temple. The Levitical priesthood performed their service to God in the temple, the sacrifices were performed on the brazen altar, and the cleansing of the priests was done at the laver. The priests did their work before the Lord around the table of showbread, the menorah, and the altar of incense. Atonement was made for the people before the Lord God in the temple. And, on the Day of Atonement the High Priest entered the Most Holy Place, also known as the Holy of Holies, of the temple to place blood on the mercy seat, the cover of the ark of the covenant.

After the temple was destroyed, the Jewish people were dispersed, and, thus, the Levitical priesthood was dismantled. The utensils used for their priestly work were plundered and taken away, probably to Rome. The rabbis then substituted a system of good deeds to replace the sacrificial system. To this day, Jews depend on their good works, the giving of charity, prayer, and daily repentance to suffice. And on the Day of Atonement they still ask for forgiveness. In their minds, blood sacrifice is not necessary, because—they reason—God knew the temple would be torn down and the sacrificial system abandoned for some time. Jewish rabbis make the assumption that, like Daniel who was in Babylonian exile, they too are in religious exile. Just as Daniel was in exile in the period between the first and second temples, religious Jews today believe they are in exile in the period between the second and third temples. Therefore, they wait and hope, depending on their good works until the Messiah they are waiting for returns to rebuild the temple and reestablish the sacrificial system.

Yet we know that the Messiah had to come before the destruction of the second temple, in order to usher in the new covenant. He became the final sacrifice, forty years before the second temple was destroyed, but will return, to rebuild the new temple and reign as king. Until then, my people hope, and we pray that their hearts will be opened to the One who became the perfect sacrifice for sin.

PRAYER

Lord Jesus, Your timing is perfect. You had to die for me before the temple was destroyed to take my sins upon Yourself, and to fulfill the sacrificial system by Your death. Please help the Jewish people to understand that no one can be saved by following the law. We are all in spiritual exile and need Your salvation. Thank You that You died for me, and help others to come to know You as well. In Your Name I pray, Amen.

TABERNACLES

I HEARD A LOUD VOICE FROM THE THRONE SAYING, "NOW THE DWELLING OF GOD IS WITH MEN, AND HE WILL LIVE WITH THEM. THEY WILL BE HIS PEOPLE, AND GOD HIMSELF WILL BE WITH THEM AND BE THEIR GOD."

REVELATION 21:3

The Feast of Tabernacles, known as Succoth or Sukkot in Hebrew, is also known as The Festival of Booths. It is the last of the three fall festivals, and is the last harvest festival of the year. It is also a festival of remembrance and celebration, something akin to America's Thanksgiving. In fact, while we cannot be certain what motivated the American Pilgrim settlers to initiate a feast of Thanksgiving, it is quite likely they consciously drew on a biblical model well known to them and cherished by them.

The Pilgrims saw themselves as new "Israelites" in a new "promised land," finding inspiration in God's Word, where the Israelites were told to celebrate "the LORD's Feast of Tabernacles" (Lev. 23:34) and to "rejoice before the LORD your God" (v. 40) at the time of the fall harvest. God told the Jewish people to "live in booths" (v. 42) in order to remember how the Israelites lived when they wandered through the wilderness.

If you were to drive through an orthodox Jewish neighborhood during the eight-day festival today, you might see a "Sukkah," or booth, in the backyard or the driveway. It is a structure usually built with wood or plastic piping, its three sides covered with cloth or lattice, and its top covered with tree branches. Inside it is decorated with fruit, and often with drawings or paper chains made by the family's children. During the celebration, branches of palm, myrtle, or poplar trees, known in Hebrew as "lulav," and a fruit from Israel known as an "etrog," are waved to the north, south, east, and west. As this is performed, a prayer of thanksgiving also is prayed, thanking the Lord for His protection and provision.

The Feast of Tabernacles not only looks back in time, remembering God's provision for the Israelites in the past, but it also looks forward. Those of us who know Jesus as the Messiah, look forward during Tabernacles to the special time when He will return to establish His kingdom—a time when we will "tabernacle" with Him forever. What a blessed thing that God would point forward to Jesus' reign through the Feast of Tabernacles!

In fact, in Zechariah we are told that when Jesus returns everyone will celebrate this feast to the Lord, in His millennial kingdom. "Then the survivors from all the nations that have attacked Jerusalem will go up year after year to worship the King, the LORD Almighty, and to celebrate the Feast of Tabernacles" (Zech. 14:16).

So if you haven't celebrated Tabernacles yet, you will one day!

PRAYER

Jesus, thank You that You are our Tabernacle—that You came to dwell with us. You dwelt among us through Your birth. And You secure me with Your eternal provision. I thank You that I dwell in You today and pray that those who don't yet know Your protection, both Jew and Gentile, will respond to Your call. In Your Name, Amen.

PURIM

ON THIS DAY THE ENEMIES OF THE JEWS HAD HOPED
TO OVERPOWER THEM, BUT NOW THE TABLES WERE
TURNED AND THE JEWS GOT THE UPPER HAND OVER
THOSE WHO HATED THEM. THESE DAYS OF PURIM
SHOULD NEVER CEASE TO BE CELEBRATED BY THE JEWS,
NOR SHOULD THE MEMORY OF THEM DIE OUT AMONG
THEIR DESCENDANTS."

ESTHER 9:1, 28

Though the Jewish people are the "apple of [God's] eye," "for whoever touches [them] touches the apple of his eye" (Zech. 2:8), they have never been "the apple of the world's eye." No, they never have been, and they never will be. The book of Esther is a great example of this, for it is the story of the Jews evil enemy, Haman, who conspired to have them totally annihilated.

"When Haman saw that Mordecai would not kneel down or pay him honor, he was enraged. Yet having learned who Mordecai's people were, he scorned the idea of killing only Mordecai. Instead Haman looked for a way to destroy all Mordecai's people, the Jews, throughout the whole kingdom of Xerxes" (Est. 3:5-6). Of course, he failed in his attempt, for he ended up losing his own life, being hung on the gallows he had prepared for Mordecai.

Today Jewish people observe Purim by reading the Book of Esther. It is a great celebration filled with festivity. As the book is read, whenever Haman's name is mentioned, the whole congregation of the synagogue will boo and make noise with noisemakers called "graggers." Yet when Mordecai's name is read, everyone will cheer and clap. Purim is a commemoration of God protecting the Jewish people, once again, from attempted annihilation—a celebration of His faithfulness to His promises and His faithfulness to the Jewish community.

We can rejoice, along with Jewish people, that Haman's plot was uncovered and thwarted. Even today, others plot to destroy the Jews and to wipe Israel off of the face of the planet. But God does not change. He protected them then, and He will protect them again.

PRAYER

I thank You God, for Your protection of the Jewish people long ago, when Haman plotted to destroy them. I know that even today there are those who desire to harm Your people and the land You gave them. I pray for their protection. And as they are attacked, I ask that You would use the turmoil to turn them to You. Help them to know that You are their God of protection. Please continue to bless and protect the people of Israel. In Messiah's name, Amen.

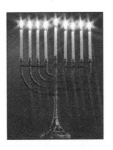

PRIDE—SEPARATING US FROM GOD

YET AT THE SAME TIME MANY EVEN AMONG THE
LEADERS BELIEVED IN HIM. BUT BECAUSE OF THE
PHARISEES THEY WOULD NOT CONFESS THEIR
FAITH FOR FEAR THEY WOULD BE PUT OUT OF THE
SYNAGOGUE; FOR THEY LOVED PRAISE FROM MEN
MORE THAN PRAISE FROM GOD.
JOHN 12:42-43

The festival of Hanukkah is also called the Festival of Miracles,
and is the celebration when the Jewish people remember how
God protected them from Syrian destruction in the second
century BC. Once the Jews were victorious, and able to rededicate the
temple from pagan desecration, the menorah, known as "ner tamid" or
eternal light, stayed lit for eight full days, when there was only enough
oil for one day. This legendary miracle is one of the miracles of God
remembered by the Jewish people during this Festival of Miracles.

For us who believe, this is further evidence of a miraculous Messiah
doing miraculous works. Yet, even profound miracles often are not
effective in changing people, for pride can keep us from seeing God's
miraculous hand at work. All humanity is separated from God because
of sin, and most sin has at least some connection to the sin of pride. In

this regard, Jewish people are no exception—no different from everyone else.

The Jewish rabbis of Jesus' day, as well as every Jewish rabbi until today, have a stake in the person of Jesus. If He is true—they are wrong! If He truly is the Messiah—they have rejected their King! If He fulfilled the prophecies of old—they have misinterpreted those prophecies! Thus, two thousand years ago, Israel, at least in part, turned its back on the Miracle Worker.

There were many Jewish leaders and Jewish people of Jesus' day who saw His miracles, witnessed His healings, and heard His message. Although they may have accepted, and even believed, some of what they saw and heard, they were unable to commit their lives to the Messiah because of their fear and pride. Like many people—like many of us today—they were intimidated and fearful. Yet is not the God of Creation as wondrous today as He was then? Of course He is. God hasn't changed, but neither has humanity. Our tendency is to miss the miraculous because we are focused on our circumstances or consumed with our own interests (pride). May God help us to see Him more clearly today.

PRAYER

Jesus, You are the Miracle Worker. Help me to see Your miracles all around me. Please help me to put aside my pride and fear to see You at work in my life. I pray for the Jewish community and Israel today—that they might see Messiah! In Your name I pray, Amen.

THEY NEED TO HEAR FROM THE CHURCH

BECAUSE OF THEIR TRANSGRESSION,
SALVATION HAS COME TO THE GENTILES
TO MAKE ISRAEL ENVIOUS.

ROMANS 1 1:1 1

Most Jewish people who come to know Jesus, do so through the witness and testimony of non-Jewish believers in Him. Most of the time, it is a Gentile friend or business associate who introduces the Jewish person to Jesus. Perhaps they invite their Jewish friend to church, to a Passion Play, or to a Christmas celebration. The fact of the matter is that initially a Gentile Christian has a less abrasive testimony than does a testimony like mine—that of a Jewish believer. Jewish people naturally assume that Gentiles are supposed to believe in Jesus. They expect Christians to go to church, and are more apt to attend a church with a Gentile Christian friend or business associate. God has put people in our lives for a purpose, and whether those people are Jewish or not, He desires for all of us to look for opportunities to engage unbelievers with the gospel of Jesus and His church.

There are those who may say that Jewish people will not go to a church. But the truth is this—Jews who are seeking certainly will. If they have questions that are spiritual in nature, and if God is working in their heart, they will go to a church—if only for a visit. Jewish people who are searching spiritually, are not searching for Jewish things. They are searching for God, for real spirituality, for the truth. They are looking to connect with the God of the universe. They are like everyone else, for they are struggling with strained marriages, health concerns, financial struggles, and raising children. It is our obligation to ask our friends, whether Jewish or not, if they want to go to church with us. Who knows what God may do? In fact, if you have a Jewish friend, ask him or her to go to church with you, and volunteer to go to synagogue with him or her. What a great way to build a bridge! Don't be afraid to ask.

PRAYER

God, give me of Your strength and boldness today. Help me to talk to my Jewish friends about You. Give me the courage to ask them questions about their life. And even if they resist, give me Your creative wisdom to explore their belief in You. Give me a burden for all those whom You have placed in my life, and the courage to reach out to them with Your love. In Your Name, Amen.

I JUST DON'T KNOW WHAT TO DO!

PREACH THE WORD; BE PREPARED IN SEASON AND
OUT OF SEASON; CORRECT, REBUKE AND
ENCOURAGE—WITH GREAT PATIENCE
AND CAREFUL INSTRUCTION.

2 TIMOTHY 4:2

What I hear from most Christians regarding speaking about Jesus to their Jewish friends—or anyone else, for that matter—is typically the same. They are afraid, feel unequipped, don't want to lose their friendships, or think people are not open to the gospel. But we must remember that God does not suggest we tell others of their need for Jesus—He commands it! We are not responsible for the results, but we are responsible for the act of sharing our faith. If we put our fear before God's command then we are making fear our god. It controls us rather than the Word of God that promises us the very words we need when we talk to others of our faith.

If we will share our faith with others in humility and gentleness, out of a concern for their spiritual and eternal life, God will honor our obedience and give us great joy. If a friendship is lost, God promises blessings for those who are rejected and hated for His Name's sake. In fact, He promises that if we leave others on account of His Name—

even family and close friends—we will be given more friends, as well as brothers and sisters, and mothers and fathers, in a spiritual sense. I have experienced this in my own life. And, if a friendship or relationship is strained because we share our faith, God is able to raise others up to share the good news, and He will renew our strength.

During the Jewish high-holiday season, my Jewish people are thinking of God's judgment on their sins, and asking Him to forgive them. But, as believers, we know that God paid for forgiveness from sin on the cross. Jesus hung on that cross and paid the penalty for our sins—for *all* the sins of *all* who believe. My people—all people—need to hear that message. Jesus came "so that [we] may know that [we] have eternal life" (1 John 5:13), and that our names are written in His book of life. My people need to hear. Your Jewish friends need to hear.

Remember—"Faith comes from hearing" (Rom. 10:17)!

PRAYER

God of the trumpet call, help me to be Your voice. May the sound of the shofar call me to urgency. Help me to wake up from my life of spiritual complacency to tell my loved ones, friends, and those who cross my path each day that Jesus is for them. He is our hope, our source of strength, our comfort, and our salvation. In a world full of death and darkness, there is hope and stability. Help me today to tell others that here is shalom—true, abiding peace— in Jesus. In Your Name, Amen.

JUST ASK

THEREFORE GO AND MAKE DISCIPLES OF ALL NATIONS,
BAPTIZING THEM IN THE NAME OF THE FATHER AND
OF THE SON AND OF THE HOLY SPIRIT, AND TEACHING
THEN TO OBEY EVERYTHING I HAVE COMMANDED YOU.
MATTHEW 28:19-20

This may sound simple, but it is not. Many Jewish people are searching and even ready to accept the Messiah. Many with whom I meet would be considered "low hanging fruit." After simply asking if they are ready to accept Jesus into their life and commit to him forever, some say, "Yes." I often wonder why no one else had ever asked them.

Perhaps they needed a Jewish person like I am from whom to hear. Perhaps God used me to put it all into perspective for them. Perhaps they needed to speak with another Jewish person before feeling comfortable with trusting Jesus for salvation. Perhaps God intended for me to pray with them. But I still cannot help but wonder whether someone else had the opportunity and missed it, or was simply too afraid to ask.

God is sovereign. Those intended for salvation will not drop through God's fingers or be lost due to human frailty or mistakes. If salvation were dependent on us, then salvation would be our responsibility. But, thankfully, it is not. God is the author of salvation and the Holy Spirit is the only One who can open blind eyes. Only Jesus sets the captive free.

And, we are not Jesus, nor the Holy Spirit.

However, that does not relieve us of our obligation to be equipped, to know the Word of God, and to be ready to ask questions, and to answer those posed to us. It is not difficult to ask questions such as, "What do you think about Jesus?" "Do you think there will ever be peace in the world … and how?" "Would you like to join me for church sometime?" "May I go with you to synagogue?" or "I have always been curious what you believe, do you think the Bible is true?"

The reason most people don't ask questions like these is that they are afraid of the answers, or afraid they will not be able to respond intelligently. Don't be afraid. Just ask. Who knows where God will take the conversation. Trust Him to guide you.

PRAYER

God, use me to speak to others. Give me the courage to ask. I want to talk to my Jewish friends, and to my non-Jewish friends about You. I confess I am afraid and need Your help, strength, and courage. I will trust Your promises to speak through me, and to give me the boldness I need. Give me someone to speak to today. In Jesus' Name, Amen.

Remain As You Are

Nonetheless, each one should retain the place
in life that the Lord assigned to him and to
which God has called him. This is the rule
I lay down in all the churches. Was a man
already circumcised when he was called? He
should not become uncircumcised. Was a man
uncircumcised when he was called?
He should not be circumcised.

1 Corinthians 7:17-18

There is beauty in the body of Messiah through ethnic and cultural diversity. As we come together from different cultural backgrounds, God is pleased. The color of our skin, the heritage we bring to worship, our languages, and our nationality is not what is significant to God. "Man looks at the outward appearance, but the LORD looks at the heart" (1 Sam. 16:7). Thus, in a spiritual sense, we are certainly all equal, separated from God because of sin, brought to new life as we trust Him, and made holy through daily worship and obedience.

At the same time, there is an important difference and distinction between Jewish people and non-Jewish people, or Gentiles, in the body of Messiah. In fact, we are given instruction to remain as we are. If an individual comes to Jesus as a Jewish person, he is not to deny his Jewish identity by becoming a non-Jew. In the same way, if a non-Jewish person trusts Jesus as Messiah, he is not to deny he is Gentile and become Jewish. God wants us to remain as we are.

There is an important reason for this biblical instruction. The Jewish people gave us Jesus, and it is the Gentile's job to take Him back to them. If Gentiles become Jewish, and Jewish people begin to deny their Jewish heritage, everything gets confused. And "God is not the author of confusion" (1 Cor. 14:33, KJV). He wants Gentiles within the body of Messiah to remain Gentile, so they may be able to provoke Jewish people to desire the Jewish Messiah, Jesus.

We should never deny our heritage. God loves us the way He made us. We were given our families for a reason, and everything has a purpose. Thank God for whom you are today. If you are not Jewish, don't desire to change. If you are Jewish, be blessed by your heritage. And together, lets proclaim the Messiah to the world!

PRAYER

Dear Lord, You created me as I am. Help me to rejoice in my position in You. I thank You that I can be Your witness in a special way, because I was created to be who I am. Help me to be a light to each and every Jewish person You bring into my life. Use me today so that others can see You through me. In Your Name, Amen.

THE MARRIAGE SUPPER

THEN THE ANGEL SAID TO ME, "WRITE: 'BLESSED ARE
THOSE WHO ARE INVITED TO THE WEDDING
SUPPER OF THE LAMB!'"
REVELATION 19:9

Have you ever been to a Jewish wedding? If not, and if you are a believer, one day you will. I hope you are ready. The Bible teaches that all of us who know Messiah Jesus are invited to one.

Jewish weddings are joyous events. According to religious Jewish custom, as well as biblical injunction, there is a wedding contract or period of betrothal, followed by the consecration ceremony when the groom comes for the bride. Finally, after the bride and groom are married, there is a great celebration—a great feast with family and friends.

As the bride and bridegroom celebrate with a joyous wedding supper, so Jesus and His bride—the church—will celebrate a marriage. Here is how John described it in Revelation: "Then I heard what sounded like a great multitude, like the roar of rushing waters and like loud peals of thunder, shouting: 'Hallelujah! For our Lord God Almighty reigns. Let us rejoice and be glad and give him glory! For the wedding of the Lamb has come, and his bride has made herself ready. Fine linen, bright and clean, was given her to wear.' (Fine linen stands for the righteous acts of the saints.) Then the angel said to me, 'Write: "Blessed are those who are invited to the wedding supper of the Lamb!'" And he added, 'These are the true words of God'" (Rev. 19:6-9).

Thus, when Jesus returns to establish His kingdom, there is going to be a great feast. The church, as the bride, is going to be united with her Bridegroom, the Messiah, forever. And His kingdom will be established, just as John wrote: "I saw the Holy City, the new Jerusalem, coming down out of heaven from God, prepared as a bride beautifully dressed for her husband" (Rev. 21:2).

Imagine that! Not only are we going to a Jewish wedding, we are going to be a part of it! Those of us who know Messiah Jesus are going to meet Him face to face, and live with Him forever, adorned in "fine linen"—beautifully dressed for our Bridegroom. Jerusalem will be adorned as well, in gold and silver, and the finest of all that creation has ever offered.

Yes, we will worship Jesus at our wedding—the wedding of the Lamb with His church—forever and ever in the new Jerusalem, the city of gold.

PRAYER

Bridegroom, I love You today, and thank You for Your love for me. I look forward to the day when I will meet You along with all the other saints to worship You in Your glory forever and ever. May the eyes of Israel be opened to who You are. May many Jewish hearts be turned to Your love, that they too may rejoice in Your kingdom and be a part of Your holy Jewish wedding, which You have prepared for all who believe in You. In Messiah's Name, Amen.

Prayer Thoughts

Prayer Thoughts

_____

_____

_____

_____

_____

_____

_____

_____

_____

_____

_____

_____

_____

PRAYER THOUGHTS

Prayer Thoughts

_____

_____

_____

_____

_____

_____

_____

_____

_____

_____

_____

_____

_____

_____

_____

_____

_____